Preaching Mark's Gospel

A Narrative Approach

Richard A. Jensen

CSS Publishing Company, Inc.
Lima, Ohio

Scripture quotations are from the *New Revised Standard Version of the Bible*, copyright 1989 by the Division of Christian Education of the National Council of the Churches of Christ in the USA. Used by permission.

Library of Congress Cataloging-in-Publication Data

Jensen, Richard A.
  Preaching Mark's Gospel : a narrative approach / Richard A. Jensen.
      p.   cm.
  Includes bibliographical references.
  ISBN 0-7880-0833-1 (pbk.)
  1. Bible. N.T. Mark — Homiletical use. 2. Bible. N.T. Mark — Criticism, Narrative.
I. Title.
BS2585.5.J47   1996
251—dc20   96-4053
                                                                                       CIP

This book is available in the following formats, listed by ISBN:
0-7880-0833-1   Book
0-7880-0834-X   IBM 3 1/2 computer disk
0-7880-0835-8   Macintosh computer disk
0-7880-0836-6   Sermon Prep

PRINTED IN U.S.A.

For Donald Juel, David Rhoads and Mary Ann Tolbert who introduced me to Mark as narrator.

Table Of Contents

Preface

The basic premise in my recent book on preaching (*Thinking in Story: Preaching In A Post-literate Age*, CSS, 1993) is that the hermeneutic of an oral culture is that teachers (rhapsode) of the tradition "think in stories." I am indebted to Prof. Thomas Boomershine, professor of New Testament at Dayton Theological Seminary, for this seminal insight.

Kenneth E. Bailey makes a similar point in his recent work titled: *Finding The Lost: Cultural Keys to Luke 15* (Concordia, 1992). In his Introduction Bailey writes:

> *At least since the fifth century B.C., and the great days of classical Greece, the Western mind has done its serious thinking in concepts. In most forms of discourse, we from the West begin with an idea and then occasionally* **illustrate** *the idea with a simile, metaphor, or parable. The conceptual language is primary and the metaphor or parable is secondary ... Middle Eastern creators of meaning do not offer a concept and then illustrate ... with a metaphor or parable. For them the equation is reversed ... The Middle Eastern mind creates meaning by the use of simile, metaphor, proverb, parable, and dramatic action. The person involved is not* **illustrating** *a concept but is rather creating meaning by reference to something concrete. The primary language is that of the metaphor/ parable and the secondary language is the conceptual interpretation of the metaphor that in Biblical literature is often given with it.*[1]

In his own way Bailey affirms the reality that "thinking in story" is the way the Middle Eastern mind, and, I would add, most oral cultures, *think*!

Preaching In Oral and Literate Cultures

In *Thinking in Story* there is laid out as an educated guess what it must have been like to take a homiletics course in a "thinking in story" culture. In this "hypothetical" course one would probably learn some or all of the following as the way of preaching:

1) The basic task of sermon construction is to stitch stories together.

2) Repetition of the basic reality of the sermon is vital if you want the hearers to remember what you have said. (The heart of any sermon ought to be the *lived reality of the gospel*, not *points about* the gospel!)

3) Begin with concrete, particular stories and then move to universal applications.

4) Stories will usually have a "tone of conflict." (This works well with a *Christus Victor* model of the saving work of Jesus Christ.)

5) The sermon is to appeal to the right brain.

6) Meaning is created through the telling of stories.

7) Sermon construction is controlled by "thinking in stories." The goal of the sermon is to invite people to *participate* in the reality of the gospel in, with and under the stories!

With the advent of literate culture this approach to preaching faded gently into the sunset. Literate culture first came to birth in ancient Greece and was propelled forward as the hermeneutic of the modern world through the invention of the printing press. Literate culture changed the basic way people think! Walter Ong has written that "writing reshapes human consciousness." "Thinking in concepts" replaced "thinking in stories" as the basic Western form of thought.

Homiletical theory changed radically with the advent of literate culture. A typical homiletics course in a literate culture makes the following kinds of points about sermon construction:

1) The basic task of sermon construction is to order *ideas* in a logical and linear way. (The sermon now becomes *points about* the gospel.)

2) Logical progression of the sermon points is the vital need.

One usually begins with an outline, which is a way of structuring ideas in space.

3) Propositions, ideas, concepts are the main points.

4) The sermon writing process *and the exegetical process* are *analytical* in nature.

5) The sermon is to appeal to the left brain.

6) The meaning of one's propositional concepts is illustrated with stories, parables, etc.

7) Sermon construction is fundamentally controlled by "thinking in concepts." The goal of the sermon is that people *understand* our ideas.

The argument of *Thinking in Story* is a simple one. It is based on the assumption that the dawn of electronic communication has relaxed the grip of literate culture on our way of seeing reality. Radio and television have replaced reading as the second most common way that we receive information. The most common way to receive information has always been face-to-face communication. Today face-to-face communication is actually threatened with demise itself from the electronic gadgetry known as *virtual reality.*

Walter Ong and others refer to electronic communication as "secondarily oral" in nature. *Sound* returns. The world of "silent print" is abrogated by the "sounded" world of radio and television. Sound, of course, was the dominant form of communication in an oral culture. For this and other reasons I have argued that preaching technique might best move forward by going *back to the future.* We can learn a lot about preaching in a world of sound from oral cultures! The above list of the characteristics of preaching in an oral culture needs to be dusted off and put to use in our new world of sound. Preaching, that is, needs to move from a world of "thinking in ideas" to a world of "thinking in stories."

Biblical Storytelling

There are, of course, many *sources* of stories for our use in preaching. We can use stories from the Bible, stories from our own autobiography, stories from church history and present tense personal stories of faith, stories from our culture (television, movies, novels, theater, popular music) and stories which we create for our own use. As I have worked with this "thinking in story" method for the past several years I have been seized by the power of biblical stories themselves as a *primary source of sermon story telling.*

Let me use the language of conversion! I have been converted! I have been converted to the power of biblical story telling. This conversion also happened to me at the feet of Tom Boomershine. At his story telling workshop, which I attended several years ago, each student was asked to memorize for oral presentation one of his or her favorite Bible stories to tell to the group on the final evening of our time together. So we did it. Twenty of us. We sat outside on the grass and told biblical stories to each other for two hours. That was one of the fastest two hours of my life! It was an incredible experience. I have always believed that the Bible is a *means of grace.* On this night several years ago I experienced the Bible as means of grace in a way that I had never experienced it before.

The most fundamental thing I learned in that story telling evening was the *power of biblical stories.* Biblical stories are dynamite. They are powerful in and of themselves. They are powerful without much explanatory help from us. They work. They do what they promise to do. Biblical stories participate in the reality of the grace which they announce.

I have put this experience of the power of biblical stories to use. In my days with Lutheran Vespers I preached countless sermons in this format, *i.e.* by simply telling biblical stories. Listener response was enthusiastic. I have preached around the country using this method. The positive response to this form of preaching has simply been overwhelming! This positive response has been just as strong from clergy with whom I have worked in enabling them to get back to the simple telling of the biblical story.

I think I learned part of the reason for the positive response to the telling of the biblical stories from a couple of retired school teachers. They liked hearing the Bible stories. "We never hear them whole!" they said. That may indeed be the heart of the matter. Laity have heard us analyze these stories and explain these stories and reduce these stories to nice points about grace, but they have not heard us tell the stories whole! When we tell the stories whole they can stand pretty much alone. How did it ever occur to us that we could improve on the story of the Prodigal Son, for example, by reducing it to ideas? Who taught us that? Why did they teach us that? When we take to explaining this or any other parable or story it ought to be powerfully clear that *analysis* of stories has replaced the *telling* of stories as the heart of the preaching.

Narrative Criticism

And now to Mark's Gospel. Mark, like the other Gospel writers and most of the Old Testament authors as well, "thinks in stories." Narrative or literary criticism is coming to understand this fact as it proposes quite new ways to approach much of biblical literature. In his work titled *The Art of Biblical Narrative*, Robert Alter proposes that a primary tool for exegesis of the biblical text is what he calls *narrative analogy.* Narrative analogy assumes that "... parallel acts or situations are used to comment on each other in biblical narrative." [2] If the biblical writers told story "b" to flesh out the reality of story "a" then perhaps we can do the same thing in our preaching!

In other words, biblical stories *talk to each other.* This is one of the ways that "thinking in stories" works. The authors of our Gospels, for example, often comment on one story by telling another story or many other stories that relate to it. A fundamental role of exegesis in approaching the Gospels, therefore, is to ask of each story if there are other stories in this Gospel which help to clarify a given text. Our exegesis, therefore, cannot just be an analysis of the verses before us. *Microscopic* exegesis of the verses for a given week is not enough. We must also engage in a kind of *panoramic* exegesis. That is, we must begin to see a given lectionary story in the light of its much larger context. We must learn to "think in stories" as we view the lectionary story for a given Sunday in the light of other Markan stories.

In another writing Robert Alter speaks of *allusion* in biblical literature. Alter writes fundamentally about the Hebrew Bible but his insights are appropriate for the world of the New Testament as well.

*Allusion, then, is not an embellishment but a fundamental
necessity of literary expression: the writer, scarcely able
to ignore the texts that have anticipated him and in some
sense given him the very idea of writing, appropriates
fragments of them, qualifies or transforms them, uses them
to give his own work both genealogy and a resonant
background ... It is just such a process of realization,
transformation, and transgression of antecedent biblical
texts ... that is constantly observable in the Bible I
want to argue for our obligation as readers to put together
the disparate pieces of biblical narrative ... [Scholarly
fixation on] dissected elements has led to a relative neglect
of the complex means used by the biblical writers* **to lock
their texts together, to amplify their meanings by linking
one text with another.** *[emphasis mine]* [3]

It is not enough to do a kind of microscopic exegesis of the
verses at hand for the assigned lectionary gospel of the week.
Gospel texts live in a world of allusion. They are often *locked
together* with other texts which help to amplify and clarify their
meaning. Those others texts to which gospel texts are locked may
be in the Old Testament or in other stories told in the Gospel as a
whole. *One way to conceive of preaching on a given gospel text,
therefore, is to tell the story of the week in the context of stories
from the Old Testament or from other sections of the same gospel!!
Preaching,* in this instance, becomes *biblical story telling.*

Narrative criticism is an emerging form of biblical understanding
which takes matters such as *narrative analogy* and *allusion*
seriously. Narrative criticism does many other things as well, but
we owe to this field of endeavor a special debt as it helps us see
narrative analogy and allusion in biblical story telling. Much of
this present work depends upon the exciting insights of narrative
critics as they take a different look at Mark's Gospel. One such
work is that by Mary Ann Tolbert, *Sowing the Gospel.* Tolbert
says that two issues motivated her decision to do her kind of
narrative analysis of the Gospel of Mark:

*... the paucity in current research of successful attempts
to interpret the Gospel* **in all its parts integrally and**

14

consistently [emphasis mine] and the prevailing judgment
of modern readers of Mark concerning its opacity,
confusion and muddle ... the tendency of modern
scholarship has been to dissolve the full narrative into
smaller, separate, and isolated units. Clearly, this
procedure mitigates against reading the text as a unified
whole.[4]

It is just this zeal to read the text as a unified whole that helps us see the Gospel of Mark as an integrated story filled with narrative analogy and allusion. Two other works have been of particular importance to this author in seeking to understand Mark as a unified narrative. These are works by Donald Juel. Juel's *Mark*, a work in the Augsburg Commentary series, and his more recent *A Master of Surprise* treat Mark as an integrated narrative and seek to understand Mark by reference to Mark as the first resort! Juel understands that Mark is a story teller and that Mark wishes us to participate in the life of his story!

Students of literature speak of the world on "this side of
the text"— the result of the communication that should
occur between narrator and listener. The effectiveness of
*the story depends upon the **involvement** [emphasis mine]*
of the reader. Though a distance exists between the world
in which Mark lived and our own, interpretations must
finally achieve some merging of those worlds, some
encounter with the "reality" Mark seeks to create with
*his story ... our primary task (therefore) is to **enter the***
***world created by the narrator**. [emphasis mine] The*
"truth" involves the words and sentences of the Gospel,
*but it is **larger than the individual parts**.*[5]

Elsewhere Juel writes that the varieties of forms of biblical criticism that have been developed in recent centuries have succeeded in distancing us from the text rather than catching us up in the life of the story at hand.

Students are not opened to the material, but are distanced
from it; they are not helped to become better interpreters,

15

but are often paralyzed by the sheer weight of scholarship. If scholarship does not produce better readers, then it is not only a waste of time but also genuinely harmful, and there are good reasons for churches to regard such scholarship with suspicion.[6]

I believe that Juel is correct in his analysis. But if this is a disaster for Bible study in general, what kind of a disaster has this created for preaching in particular? As suggested earlier, literate culture led homiletics away from story telling as a way of inviting our *participation* in the text to analysis of bits of texts which provide us with meanings, propositions and ideas. The traditional commentaries have propelled us into thinking that gleaning ideas from this word discovery or that source discovery or a new textual discovery makes for good sermons. From the disassembled parts of the text we find points and meanings for our sermons. That's fine if our assumption is that the Gospel of Mark, for example, is written to communicate these bits and pieces of dissected and disassembled information. If the narrative critics are right, however, and Mark has a story to tell which invites us into its reality, then our brilliant bits and pieces of information lead us far astray from biblical intent!

Methodology

The method of this volume will be to take the assigned Markan pericopes in their *Markan order* (!) and seek to place these stories in the larger story of Mark, looking for things like narrative analogy and allusion. You will still need your normal commentaries for study and analysis of the text. This work does not replace the need for such biblical tools. This work, rather, has the following purposes:

1. To call us beyond analysis of bits of information into the larger world of Mark's story.

2. To invite us to preach on Mark's Gospel at times and perhaps quite often by putting individual Markan texts in the context of Mark's larger story.

3. To invite us to become Markan story tellers inviting hearers to participate in Mark's story in such a way that the story begins to lay hold of them as it seeks to change their life in light of the presence of Jesus Christ.

In taking up this task I am deeply indebted to scholars such as Donald Juel, David Rhoads, Jack Dean Kingsbury, Mary Ann Tolbert, Werner Kelber and others for helping me to see narrative analogy, allusion, the big picture as Mark tells it. I am not a Markan expert myself. Like most preachers I must depend upon the "experts" for much of what I know in these matters. What I can do and hope to do in this work is to pass on what I have been taught about Mark's gospel in ways that might be of help to you in the preaching task. Very little work has been done thus far in seeking to apply the insights of narrative criticism to the task of preaching. I hope this work begins to fill this gap and that many biblical scholars will arise who can help us make the bridge between a narrative understanding of a Gospel like Mark and our homiletical challenge.

The Gospel of Mark

In the past few centuries scholars have created a variety of approaches to the study of the Gospels in general and Mark in particular. A very brief history of the ways in which the Gospel of Mark has been read and interpreted is given in the first chapter of a book edited by Janice Capel Anderson and Stephen D. Moore titled *Mark & Method.*[7] The first and introductory chapter of their work is "The Lives of Mark." The authors trace the history of the interpretation of Mark from the earliest days in the church where Mark was understood to be a scribe of Peter through many other possible readings of Mark. In this brief history they feature the ways in which Mark has begun to be seen as a *narrator.* There is a story being narrated here! One must never get so lost in the details of the stories or an interest in Mark's sources or a passion for the establishment of the rightful text of Mark that one forgets that Mark is a storyteller! The evangelists, they maintain, are narrative thinkers, narrative theologians.

Werner Kelber has picked up this interest in Mark as narrator of story in his *Mark's Story of Jesus*. He notes that Mark refers to his story as "gospel" in the very first verse of his work:

> *As far as is known, this is the first time in early Christian literature that a story about Jesus' life and death is written down under the title "gospel."... In view of the traditional oral nature of gospel, Mark's concept must be considered a significant departure from early Christian usage of gospel. By writing a story and calling it gospel Mark inspires people to read his gospel story ... There is only one way to understand Mark's gospel message, and that is to read his whole story from 1:1 to 16:8.*[8]

Chapter 2 of this work by Anderson and Moore is written by Elizabeth Struthers Malbon and is titled "How Does the Story Mean?" Her article touches briefly on those matters that are of deep concern to narrative readers: implied author and reader, the characters, the setting and the plot. Under the heading of "Rhetoric" Ms. Malbon asserts that

> *Markan rhetoric is narrative rhetoric. By the way the story is told, the implied author persuades the implied reader first to understand and then to share and extend the story's levels of meaning. Mark's rhetoric is one of juxtaposition — placing scene over against scene in order to elicit comparison, contrast, insight. This juxtaposition includes repetition, not only of scenes but also of words and phrases ... Juxtaposition also includes intercalation — splicing one story into another — and framing — placing similar stories at the beginning and the end of a series. In addition juxtaposition includes foreshadowing and echoing of words, phrases, and whole events. Echoing and foreshadowing may be intratextual (within the text) or intertextual (between texts).*[9]

Mary Ann Tolbert is one of today's narrative critics who seeks to understand the Gospel of Mark in a comprehensive way. She writes, "I am firmly convinced that the study of any individual pericope is best carried out with some sense of the total narrative context in which it appears ...."[10] Her goal is "... to articulate at least one possible 'consistent interpretation' of 'the Gospel in all its parts,' using the perspectives and tools provided by literary criticism as the practical basis of analysis."[11]

In her thorough analysis of Mark, Tolbert has become convinced that the Gospel of Mark belongs to the literary genre of popular culture and popular literature of its time. She sees similarities between Mark and the ancient erotic novel though Mark is clearly not of this type. Her point is that Mark's stories work together in ways that its ancient *hearers* (Gospels were written to be read aloud) would have been able to follow and understand. Tolbert reaches the following conclusions in her attempt to understand the genre of Mark's Gospel:

> *While the Gospel of Mark and the early examples of the ancient novel obviously do not share the same story line, their rhetorical, stylistic, and linguistic similarities are conspicuous. Both are synthetic, conventional narratives that combine historiographic form with epic and dramatic substance. Episodic plots, central turning points, final recognition sequences, dialogic scenes with narrative frames, sparing but crucial use of monologue, repetition, narrative summaries, foreshadowing, and monolithic, illustrative characters are some of the elements the Gospel and ancient novels have in common.*[12]

Tolbert is interested in two realities here. In the first place, if Markan rhetoric shares similarities with the rhetoric of the popular culture of its times, then the first hearers of this Gospel have a great advantage over us in hearing the story as it was told. Secondly, this fact would also explain why it is so difficult for us today to crack Mark's narrative code. Tolbert precisely proposes to help us crack this code and enable us to hear and read this Gospel in a new way.

One of the realities of this ancient rhetorical world is that the concern of an audience is not in *what* will happen but *how* it will

19

happen. Ancient story tellers, therefore, often provided their hearers with plot synopses in order to aid the hearing of the tale. Tolbert sees the Parable of the Sower in Mark 4:3-8, 14-20 and the Parable of the Tenants in Mark 12:1-11 functioning as the plot synopses of the first and second halves of Mark's Gospel respectively. Here we come to our first serious crisis in a narrative approach to preaching Mark's Gospel. *Neither of these parables identified as the plot synopses of this Gospel appear in the lectionary cycle!* We will have to bring these stories into consideration for a narrative approach to preaching Mark. In our preaching itself these stories will need to be told and perhaps re-told many times in the course of the lectionary year.

The Parable of the Sower

A few comments on the Parable of the Sower will be helpful in advance of our pericope by pericope walk through Mark. Tolbert is convinced that as a plot synopsis of the first part of Mark's Gospel this parable functions as an allegory. She thinks the same is true of the use of the Parable of the Tenants in the second part of the Gospel. Tolbert writes, "... the clearest evidence of the centrality of the parable of the Sower comes in the words of the character Jesus himself: 'Do you not understand this parable? How then will you understand all the parables?' (4:13) ...[This parable] appears to reflect the basic actions of Jesus and the other characters in its respective division [of the Gospel]."[13] Tolbert is convinced that the Parable of the Sower is a guide as to how the first part of Mark is to be understood. With respect to Jesus we understand that he is the Sower of the Word. The parable is a clue to the identity of Jesus.

Furthermore, the parable defines for us the roles of many of the other characters in Mark. There will be at least four kinds of characters in this story corresponding to the four types of soil. Remember: this parable which is allegorical in nature is a plot synopsis. Once we have heard it and heard it again (for it is told twice) we have been alerted to at least four kinds of hearers who will appear in this story with Jesus.

1. The first kind of hearers of the word are like seeds sown on a path. They get devoured instantly by the birds (4:4). In his explanation of the parable to the disciples (4:14-20) Jesus says that it is Satan who comes immediately to take away the seed sown in these hearers.

2. The second kind of hearers of the word are rocky ground. The seed takes immediate root, springs up, but because it has no depth it withers away (4:5-6). In his explanation of the parable Jesus calls these hearers those who hear with joy the sowing of the word but have no root in themselves. They endure for just a short time and when tribulation or persecution arises on account of the word, they fall away (Mark 4:16-17).

3. The third group of hearers of the word to expect in Mark are those who can be compared to seed sown in thorns which is therefore choked up (4:7). Jesus explains that these kinds of hearers are too much enamored by the cares of the world and a delight in riches. These cares eventually choke the growth of the word so that these hearers are left unfruitful (Mark 4:18-19).

4. The final type of hearers that we will meet in this story is the good soil. They bring forth grain growing up and increasing thirtyfold, sixtyfold and a hundredfold (Mark 4:8). Jesus explains that these are those who hear the word and accept it and bear fruit (Mark 4:20).

Tolbert is not the first nor the last biblical scholar to attach central importance to the Parable of the Sower in Mark's Gospel. Juel indicates that this parable of Jesus in Mark tells us how it is with Jesus and how it shall be.

> *The parables make a considerable difference to the overall narrative not by motivating action but by offering a brief plot synopsis and a forecast that keeps the reader's attention directed at the road ahead. **The story unfolds precisely as the parable promises.** [emphasis mine] ... The narrative picks up the imagery and develops it — although not in terms of some clear structure in the Gospel, as though each section of the Gospel represented some stage in the parable ... The parables introduce momentum into the story that drives beyond the ending*

into the future when the results of Jesus' planting must begin to emerge. The parables make no demands, only promises that must be borne out in the narrative ... .[14]

We have been alerted, therefore, to a fundamental reality of Mark's narrative. A parable such as the Parable of the Sower is not just an interesting story to be analyzed, understood and preached upon in its own terms. We must, rather, be constantly on the lookout as we hear and read this story as to how individuals and their response to the One Who Sows the Word carry out the plot of Mark's Gospel. We now, with our ancient readers, know the basic outline of the story of the first ten chapters of the Gospel. The suspense for us is not *what* will occur. We know what is going to occur. The parable tells us so! What we don't know is *how* it is going to happen. Perhaps even more importantly we don't know which kind of soil we are or which kind of soil our parishioners shall be as they hear the story of the One Who Sows the Word.

It might be helpful for you to know in advance how Tolbert applies the parable/plot synopsis of the Gospel. She maintains that the Pharisees are the first type of hearers. We first meet the Pharisees in four consecutive controversy stories told in Mark 2:15—3:6. Satan is at work mightily as they reject the Sower out of hand.

She identifies the second type of hearer with the disciples. They hear the word gladly and it takes root until trials and tribulations beset them. We are reminded in advance of the dim view of the disciples portrayed in the Gospel of Mark.

Tolbert proposes the rich young ruler as the model of the third kind of hearer (Mark 10:17-31). The rich young ruler has a sincere desire to inherit eternal life. He has kept the commandments. But he cannot give up his riches. The cares and pleasures of this life finally choke the growth of the word. King Herod might also be this type of hearer (Mark 6:14-29). Herod feared John the Baptist and heard him gladly! Herod was sorry for his oath to give Herodias what she wanted — namely John the Baptist's head on a platter. But because of his oath and his guests, because of the cares and pleasures of life, the word was choked out of Herod's life as well. Pilate also appears to fit this category (Mark 15:1-15). It is clear in

22

the story that Pilate wants to release Jesus for whatever reasons. Has he, too, heard the word with sympathetic ears? Finally, to satisfy the crowd (bending to the cares and pleasures of the world), Pilate hands Jesus over for crucifixion.

Finally, Tolbert proposes that those who are healed are the faithful ones who reap thirtyfold, sixtyfold and hundredfold. We hear the story of three such persons immediately following the telling of the parable in Mark 4. Mark 5:1-20 is a lengthy narration of the healing of the Gerasene demoniac. This is followed by the stories of the healing of the daughter of Jairus and the woman with the flow of blood (Mark 5:21-43). The word of the Sower takes such deep root in the lives of these persons that they are healed in body and spirit. Those who are healed in the stories told in Mark 5 are people who hear and believe and whose lives bear fruit, thirtyfold, sixtyfold and hundredfold. And just look at these candidates for the good soil prize! A Gerasene demoniac. A ruler of the synagogue. An unclean woman. If such persons are "good soil" people, might we not have a shot at being a "good soil" person as well?! There is much good news, much gospel, in the stories of good soil in Mark 5!

Implications For Preaching

This kind of hearing/reading of Mark's Gospel in general and the Parable of the Sower in particular has tremendous implications for the task of preaching. There is much of "narrative analogy" and "allusion" here. These stories do talk to each other! Many of the stories in Mark's Gospel seem to be locked in to this parable of the Sower. Preaching that "thinks in story" will follow this lead. There are many Markan stories that can be stitched together in our sermons. Sometimes these Markan stories can be "stitched together" with very little exposition from those of us who preach. The stories interpret each other. Even more importantly, the stories interpret us!

This is the kind of help that I hope to offer you in the pages of this book. As we take up the lectionary pericopes one by one we will look for their narrative connectedness to Mark's story. That will be the first task of each chapter. A second task will be to provide "Homiletical Directions" on how Markan stories might be stitched together. As suggested in the above paragraph, there will be times when this is sufficient. The stories will do their own sowing of gospel seed on the hearts of our listeners. At other times a *living center of proclamation* will be recommended.

Reference has been made to the *living center.* What is meant by this is that at the center of our sermon we "speak for God" or "speak for Jesus" in first person, present tense language. Ideas will not suffice as the center for biblically narrative sermons. To reduce finally all of our story telling into ideas subverts the entire narrative process.

At the center of the sermon, rather, there ought to be a living center! One of the ways to define a biblical narrative sermon structure is to describe it as *one to four biblical stories on the way to, or gathered around, a living center.* Proclamation, not ideas, should be the heart of the sermonic matter. By proclamation I want to underline the *good news character of preaching.* The good news of God's incredible love for sinful human beings is the *only unique message we have to announce and proclaim to our people each week.*

When we look together at these Markan texts we want to ask what good news is spoken here from God or through Jesus that we can in turn proclaim to our hearers. When we bring forth this good news we will speak it in first person, present tense language. We don't say: "What we learn from the Parable of the Sower is that Jesus will sow the good seed on every heart." That's true, of course. But it is true in this sentence as *information.* Let's make it a statement of *proclamation.* We say instead: "Jesus says to us today through this parable: 'I am the Sower of the Word. I have come to sow the word on every kind of human soil. I have come to sow the word on the soil of your heart.' "

First person language! Present tense! And thus we *speak for God.* Thus we make promises to all who will listen. Thus we become, in our turn, Sowers of the Word. Our prayer is that the Holy Spirit can take our words on the longest journey imaginable. Our prayer is that the Holy Spirit can take our words all the way from human ears to human hearts. Our prayer is that the Holy Spirit can take our proclamation and create faith where fear once reigned. Oh, it is a delightfully wondrous business, this sowing the seed of the gospel!

---

1. Kenneth E. Bailey, *Finding the Lost: Cultural Keys to Luke 15* (St. Louis: Concordia, 1992), pp. 15, 16.

2. Robert Alter, *The Art of Biblical Narrative* (Basic Books, 1981), p. 7.

3. Robert Alter, *The World of Biblical Literature* (Basic Books, 1992), pp. 108-109.

4. Mary Ann Tolbert, *Sowing the Gospel: Mark's World in Literary-Historical Perspective* (Minneapolis: Fortress Press, 1989), p. 80.

5. Donald H. Juel, *Mark*, Augsburg Commentary on the New Testament (Minneapolis: Augsburg, 1990), pp. 13-14.

6. Donald H. Juel, *A Master of Surprise: Mark Interpreted* (Minneapolis: Fortress Press, 1994), p. 6.

7. Janice Capel Anderson and Stephen D. Moore, *Mark & Method: New Approaches in Biblical Studies* (Minneapolis: Fortress, 1992), pp. 1-22.

8. Werner H. Kelber, *Mark's Story of Jesus* (Philadelphia: Fortress Press, 1979), p. 16.

9. Anderson and Moore, *op. cit.*, p. 34.

10. Tolbert, *op. cit.*, p. xii.

11. Tolbert, *op. cit.*, p. 3.

12. Tolbert, *op. cit.*, p. 78.

13. Tolbert, *op. cit.*, p. 122.

14. Juel, *op. cit.*, p. 57.

Mark 1:1-8

Seven of the Lectionary B pericopes from Mark's Gospel come from the first chapter of Mark! Several of these pericopes overlap each other. Where there is overlapping you may wish to consult other sections of this work for additional comments. For the Baptism of our Lord Sunday, for example, the appointed text is Mark 1:4-11, which overlaps with the final four verses of the pericope for the Second Sunday in Advent.

The title or heading of Mark's Gospel is stated simply: "The beginning of the good news of Jesus Christ, the Son of God" (1:1). And then the story begins. It begins, so to speak, in the middle of time. No genealogies here. Mark gets right down to the business of announcing the identity of his central figure. Jesus is the Christ, the Son of God. Jack Dean Kingsbury has written an important treatise on the Christology of Mark's Gospel.[1] Kingsbury's primary argument throughout the book is that Mark understands Jesus to be the Son of God. He sees that this revelation of Jesus as Son of God comes in stages. Mark 1:1 begins as the story of the Son of God. Mark 1:11 is the culmination of the first part of Mark's story as God in heaven identifies Jesus as "beloved Son." Kingsbury maintains that Mark writes the Gospel in such a way that Jesus' identity is revealed in stages. In Mark 8:29 Peter will confess that Jesus is the Messiah. In 10:47-48 blind Bartimaeus appeals to Jesus as Son of David. Finally, and very importantly, the centurion declares Jesus to be Son of God. Mark 15:39. Kingsbury asserts that the confession of the centurion is as important as the baptismal proclamation of God to Jesus in baptism (1:11) and on the mountain of transfiguration (9:7) in establishing Jesus' identity.

Mark's opening name for Jesus is Jesus Christ. The reference to Christ is a reference to the Messiah promised to Israel by the prophet Nathan speaking to David. (See 2 Samuel 7:4-17.) It is this promise of God to David which fueled Israel's hopes and expectations for the 1,000 years between the time of David and the time of Jesus. "Are you the One who is to come or do we look for another?" (See Matthew 11:1-6; Luke 7:18-23.) These were the words on the lips of the people of Israel as each new leader arose. Mark makes it very clear, therefore, that this old promise is now fulfilled. Jesus is the Christ/Messiah.

Mark's Gospel begins with a clarion call! Here is Jesus Christ, the Son of God. It ends, however, in a whisper — in the fear of the women at the tomb.

Whereas v.1 is the heading or title of this Gospel, vv. 1-13 may serve as a prologue to the entire narrative. In these few verses Jesus' identity and authority is confirmed by quoting the Hebrew Bible (vv. 2-3); by prophetic announcement (vv. 7-8); by a voice from heaven (v. 11); and by cosmic and apocalyptic signs (vv. 12-13). This voice from heaven is heard again in Mark 9:7. Jesus is clearly the center of the story that is to come!

The action takes place in Galilee (v. 9). Mark's story begins and ends in Galilee! At the close of the story the young man at the tomb announces that Jesus' followers are to go to Galilee to see him even as he told you. Jesus told the disciples this during the night of prayer at the Mount of Olives. "... After I am raised up, I will go before you to Galilee" (Mark 14:28). Geography plays an important part in the story of Mark's Gospel. The first ten chapters of the story take place in Galilee and focus on Jesus, the Sower of the Word. In Galilee, that is, Jesus is primarily the preacher spreading the good news of the coming of the kingdom. We hear quite often that this reality is to be kept a *secret*.

Beginning with the Palm Sunday story in Mark 11:1-11 the story shifts to Jerusalem where Jesus, the son of the owner of the vineyard, will be killed. (See Mark 12:1-11.) In Jerusalem Jesus is *openly* proclaimed as the Christ. The secret is out! The tragedy begins! (See Jesus' own predictions of his passion: Mark 8:31-32; 9:30-31; 10:32-34.)

Following the heading of the Gospel there comes a quotation from the prophet Isaiah. There is a problem here in that this quotation cannot be found in this form in Isaiah! The quotation, rather, appears to combine Exodus 23:20, Malachi 3:1 and Isaiah 40:3. Mary Ann Tolbert in her *Sowing the Gospel* notes that whatever its source the quotation seems to be a fine summary of the themes which Mark associates with the ministry of Jesus. She presents an elaborate argument to make the case that this quotation from the Hebrew Bible is about Jesus, not John the Baptist. The Baptist's story begins in v. 4. Verses 1-3 should be read as pertaining to Jesus and setting forth the themes of his ministry. Jesus is the One sent by God as a messenger who will sow the word. He is the One "on the way" to Jerusalem: Mark 8:27; 9:33-34; 10:32. Jesus is also the One who calls us to follow him on the way to Jerusalem and the cross: Mark 9:34-38; 10:21, 52. Jesus first meets John in the wilderness. Furthermore, Jesus spends much of his ministry in the wilderness: Mark 1:35, 45; 6:31-32, 35; 8:4. "Throughout the sowing of the word, Jesus repeatedly embodies 'the voice of one crying in the wilderness' (1:3)."[2]

With the appearance of John the Baptist in v. 4 the story moves to its human side. We have had the introduction to the Divine Sower. How shall it be with people on the earth? John calls upon the people to repent and be baptized for the forgiveness of their sins. The clues to the identity of John point also to the fulfillment of promises of old. John was clothed in camel's hair, had a leather girdle about his waist and ate locusts and wild honey. This is precisely the clothing and the diet of Elijah the prophet as reported in 2 Kings 1:8. Here is narrative analogy. The ministry of John the Baptist is linked with that of Elijah. The two are to be understood in relation to each other. There was the expectation that Elijah would come again before the days of the Christ. The allusions in these first chapters of Mark never seem to end!

John recognizes in his preaching that he is not the One who is to come. "I have baptized you with water; but he will baptize you with the Holy Spirit" (Mark 1:8). Such is John's promise. But the story breaks off before Jesus baptizes anyone. This story lays before us a promise that is not fulfilled with any immediacy. Perhaps it is the very ministry of Jesus that is the fulfillment of this promise. It does happen with immediacy that the Spirit descends upon Jesus in the form of a dove. Jesus appears as the Spirit's man, as God's man in Galilee. His is a ministry animated by the very breath (spirit) and life of God!

We shall say more about the baptism of Jesus in chapter 2.

The Life Giver, the Son of God, is ready to begin his ministry. The story of Jesus will begin with a rush of life-giving events: an unclean spirit is cast out (1:21-28), Simon's mother-in-law is healed from a fever (1:29-31), demons are cast out (1:35-39); a leper is cleansed (1:40-45) and a paralytic is forgiven and healed (2:1-12). Such events mark the ministry of Jesus through the first ten chapters of Mark's Gospel.

Homiletical Directions

There is an embarrassment of riches for the story telling preacher in these few verses. One might take the opening quotation from the Hebrew Bible (vv. 2-3) and tell the story of the source(s) of this quote. Secondly, one can show that the ministry of Jesus takes up the themes of these verses. This will serve as a kind of introduction to Mark's story of Jesus. There is much good news that can be proclaimed from such stories.

Or, one might focus one's stories around John the Baptist. Story One might be the story of Elijah which sets the scene and establishes the importance of John's ministry. Story Two can center on John's baptismal ministry and his pointing to another who will baptize with the Holy Spirit. Story Three can tell some or all of the healing stories in Mark 1 and 2, demonstrating the life-giving ministry of the One who is filled with the Spirit. Many of these stories do occur in the Epiphany cycle of Markan texts, so we may not want to touch them yet at this point. The living center of proclamation might center on Jesus who says in effect: "I have been baptized with the Spirit, the very life of God. I offer you this life. I have been baptized that I might send forth your unclean spirits. I have been baptized that I might cleanse you of all that ails you. I have been baptized that I might forgive you all your sins."

It might be best that on this first Sunday in Cycle B that uses a Markan text, we preach, a sermon which introduces the full range of this Gospel. Let's focus on v. 1, the very title of Mark's Gospel:

"This is the beginning of the gospel of Jesus the Messiah, the Son of God."

Story One will tell the story of the promise to David by Nathan from 2 Samuel 7:4-17. Other materials from 2 Samuel might be needed to set that story in proper context. Our living center can arise out of the telling of this story. God speaks through Nathan to David in this passage. God says: "I will raise up a Messiah from the offspring that follow you. I will establish the throne of his kingdom forever. I will offer to your people eternal hope."

Story Two can tell how the people of Israel longed for this promise to be fulfilled for 1,000 years. The people of Israel waited. Waiting is a good Advent theme. As each new leader arose in Israel the question on the lips of the people was: "Are you the One who is to come or do we look for another?" Matthew (11:1-6) and Luke (7:18-23) tell the story in such a way that this question is addressed to Jesus. Mark cuts right to the heart of the matter. Verse 1 rings out with the sound of the trumpet: "The beginning of the good news of Jesus Christ ...." Mark has been empowered to announce what he has experienced for himself. Mark has experienced the One who announces, "I am the Messiah. I am the Christ. I come to bring God's eternal kingdom. I come to bring you eternal hope."

Story Three can introduce the Parable of the Sower. We pointed out in the Preface the importance of this parable in Mark's Gospel. Why not call it forth on this first Sunday in Mark's Gospel? Through this parable of Jesus, Mark indicates to us that there are at least four kinds of soil, four kinds of responses to Jesus' sowing of the seed; to Jesus' announcement that he is the Messiah. (See the Preface for a discussion of these four types of hearers.) The whole issue of hearing is important for us. We have heard Jesus' announcement that he is the Messiah. And how shall we hear? We will relive the story of Messiah's birth in just a few weeks. How shall we hear?

Story Four can briefly touch on the last story in Mark's Gospel. The Gospel that began with a trumpeted announcement (1:1) ends with a whisper (16:8). The women were afraid. Trembling and astonishment had come upon them. They said nothing to anyone.

31

Our sermon may conclude something like this: "Mark's Gospel begins with a trumpet. The Jesus introduced to us by Mark would say to us: 'I am the Christ. I am the Messiah. I come to bring God's eternal kingdom to you. I come to bring you eternal hope.' Will we today move away from this message in fear and astonishment? Will we move away from this message with a whisper? Or will we move away from this message as those convinced of its trumpet sound? May the Holy Spirit empower us to believe the word of this Messiah Christ. May the Holy Spirit empower us to sound forth the trumpet of good news to all whom we meet. Amen"

A procedural footnote: In our biblical storytelling we might choose occasionally to craft one of our biblical stories for telling to the children. This would be a wonderful use of the "Children's Sermon." Tell them a Bible story. Tell them a Bible story that is one of the stories of the day's sermon.

---

1. Jack Dean Kingsbury, *The Christology of Mark's Gospel* (Philadelphia: Fortress Press, 1983).

2. Mary Ann Tolbert, *Sowing The Gospel: Mark's World in Literary-Historical Perspective* (Minneapolis: Fortress Press, 1989), p. 245.

Mark 1:4-11

We will focus our attention here on verses 9-11. In his *Mark* and *A Master of Surprise* Donald Juel sees the *tearing open of the heavens* in v. 10 as one of the keys to the entire book of Mark. Before turning to his insights on v. 10 we'll look briefly at the other verses in this short segment in Mark's Gospel. Mark tells us that Jesus came from Nazareth in Galilee. We pointed out in chapter 1 that Galilee is a crucial geographical aspect of the structure of Mark. Chapters 1-10 of this Gospel take place in Galilee, chapters 11-16 in Jerusalem.

The voice from heaven is also an important key to Mark's narrative. We will hear this voice speaking forth the same words in the Transfiguration story in Mark 9:2-8. (See especially v. 7.) In each place Jesus is designated as the beloved son of God. These words are probably an allusion to Psalm 2:7 in the Hebrew Bible. This is a Royal Psalm in which God speaks to his "anointed" as a "son." The people of Israel in the first century probably regarded this Psalm as a kind of prophecy of David's son who would arise to save Israel. When a voice from heaven speaks to Jesus saying these words, the meaning for first century Jews was locked in to their understanding of this Psalm. Psalm 2 and Mark 1 are in conversation with each other.

The words "with you I am well pleased" seem to be an allusion to Isaiah 42:1: "Here is my servant, whom I uphold, my chosen, in whom my soul delights; I have put my spirit upon him; he will bring forth justice to the nations." The narrative analogy here would lead us to believe that Jesus is to be seen, therefore, as the One who brings *justice* to the world.

Juel suggests that there might also be a reference in these verses to the "beloved son" whom Abraham was asked to sacrifice on Mount Moriah (Genesis 22:1-18). This old story of Abraham and

33

Isaac was central to Jewish identity. The original hearers of these words might have already begun to think that as "Beloved Son" this Jesus was also destined to be offered up[1] (cf. Romans 8:32). Christian identity is to be bound up with a sacrifice that God, finally, could not ask Abraham to make but which God did make with God's own son!

It would not be difficult in a sermon, therefore, to tell one or more of the stories from the Hebrew Bible which are allusions to the words of the voice from heaven. Such a sermon could proceed to lay out the nature of Jesus' ministry in Mark's Gospel as the "beloved son" who is the Christ, who is the Son of God (see also Mark 1:1; 9:7; 15:39), who seeks to bring justice to the nations as he gives his life as a ransom for many (10:45).

What is ironic about the appearance of this beloved son is its setting. Jesus shows up to inaugurate his ministry in the wilderness among sinners who are being called to repent of their sins. Jesus seems to be in the wrong place with the wrong people. This is not the last time that Mark uses such irony to underscore an important reality concerning this Son of God.

And now to the rending of the heavens. Matthew and Luke use a Greek word for the rending of the heavens which means that the heavens were "opened." The Greek word that Mark uses, however, is more like a radical *schism*, a tearing open, a dynamic and final rending. This rending creates an interesting structure in Mark's Gospel. Here the heavens are opened and the spirit descends upon Jesus. At the end of the story Jesus breathes his last (that is, he gives up his spirit) and the curtain of the temple is *schismed*, ripped in two from the top to the bottom. In the very next verse the centurion makes his confession: "Truly this man was God's Son!" (Mark 15:37-39). (See also Hebrews 10:19-25.)

Juel gives his most expanded analysis of this "tearing open" in Chapter 3 of his *A Master of Surprise*. He maintains that these parallel passages in Mark 1:9-11 and 15:37-39 form an *inclusion*: a pattern that begins with Jesus' baptism and ends with his death. Juel interprets this tearing open as God breaking down the protective barriers between the divine and the human. God is no longer to be confined to some safe sacred space. God is now loose and at work in the world of common humanity.

Mark's narrative is about the intrusion of God into a world that has become alien territory — an intrusion that means both death and life. That the author allows such associations suggests that something holds the story together, but that little explicit help will be given in making the connections. Reading will require imagination and involvement ... .[2]

There is, perhaps, a third story of schism and tearing open told in Mark 14:3-8. An unnamed woman *breaks open* an alabaster jar of ointment and pours it over Jesus' head. It may be true of this passage also that barriers between the divine and the human are broken down. The unnamed woman performs a *prophetic action* which anoints this human one, Jesus, as God's divinely sent Messiah. Truly God is no longer to be confined to some safe sacred place. The entire system of holy management of divine realties is being ripped apart. God is loose in this world, and this woman knows it! She even senses that Jesus' death, for which she anoints his body beforehand, is the fulfillment of his ministry. This is precisely the point that the disciples, in the story told by Mark, can never figure out.

The theme that Juel develops for understanding the rending of the heavens and the temple curtain is that of *transgressing boundaries.* Mark's opening chapters are filled with ritual imagery that deals largely with matters of purity. In his first public act, Jesus is confronted by an unclean spirit in a holy place (1:21-28). Jesus drives the spirit out, yet in doing so he initiates a ministry in which he will himself violate ritual boundaries. He acts with unprecedented authority, not like the scribes (1:22, 27). In the scenes that follow Jesus touches a leper (1:40-45), eats with the unwashed (2:15-17), heals on the Sabbath (3:1-6), even justifies his disciples' plucking grain on the Sabbath (2:23-28). And in his declaration to the paralytic — "Your sins are forgiven" (2:5) — he violates perhaps the most important boundary of all, the one separating God from the created order.[3]

In his forgiving of sinners Jesus had transgressed the boundary between what God can do and what humans can do. For this he is charged with blasphemy by the bystanding scribes (2:7). That's how the story opens and that's how the story ends. Before the high priest and all the chief priests and the elders and the scribes, Jesus was charged with blasphemy (14:53-65, note v. 64). God was loose in the world. Religious boundaries were being shattered. Surely the One who does such things, the One accused of blasphemy, must die. And so he did. The story, however, does not end with his death. The story ends with the women at the tomb. And a young man said: "Do not be alarmed; you are looking for Jesus of Nazareth, who was crucified. He has been raised; he is not here" (Mark 16:6). Risen indeed! The bands of death have been *torn* and Jesus is loose in the world once again!

Homiletical Directions

It has already been indicated above that biblical stories on the Son of God motif in Mark would be one way to move with this text. The living center could work at making the proclamation of God to Jesus become a proclamation of Jesus *to us*. Stories from the Hebrew Bible and from Mark can set up God's proclamatory word: "You are my Son, the Beloved; with you I am well pleased" (Mark 1:11). A transition needs to be made so that these words of God to Jesus can be heard as Jesus' word to us. It ought not be difficult, for example, to hear this word as a word addressed to all of us in our baptism! In and through the event of our baptism God has addressed us. "You are my children. I am pleased with you." God in Jesus Christ says this very same word to us today!

Let me sketch in a bit broader detail a possible way to treat the schism-in-the-heavens reality so important to Juel. Story One can be the story of the text, focusing attention on the tearing open of the heavens and establishing the reality that God is now loose in the world of common humanity. To show the importance of this story in Mark it would be well to tell the Mark 15:37-39 story here as well. You may wish to close this theme of God loose in the world with the story of the resurrection in Mark 16. At any rate, the thrust of this story or stories would be to catch the sense of God at work among us.

Story Two would deal with the reality that the God who is loose in Jesus is a God who breaks down barriers and transgresses boundaries. That is true already in v.10 as God shatters the boundary that separates the divine and the human. Several stories that follow in Mark can be used to develop this motif. In two stories (1:21-28 and 1:40-45) Jesus breaks down the barrier between the clean and the unclean. In 2:1-11 Jesus breaks down the barrier between sinners and God. Several other stories that fit this theme have been alluded to above. We should probably not omit from the breaking of barriers motif the reality that Jesus also breaks down the barrier between death and life.

Story Three might be the story of the unnamed woman. This, too, is a boundary-breaking story. Our focus might be on the death and life boundary. The woman anoints Jesus for death. Death will be the last step on Jesus' journey to resurrection and the giving of new life. God's Kingdom has come indeed!

The living center of proclamation in the telling of these stories would be a word from Jesus.

"I am God loose in the world. I have come to break down the barriers that separate you from God. I have come to break down the uncleanness that separates you from God. You are clean!" (Mark 1:21-28).

"I have come to break down the diseases which separate you from God. You are whole!" (Mark 1:32-34, 40-45).

"I have come to break down the power of the sins that cut you off from your Creator. Your sins are forgiven" (Mark 2:1-12).

"I have come to break down the power of death that has had the ultimate power to separate you from God. I give you life forever" (Mark 16:1-8).

These proclamatory words can be spoken one at a time as you tell the relevant stories. Or you can save them until the end. Or you can both say the single lines with the appropriate story *and* put them all together in a summarizing climax.

---

1. Donald Juel, *Mark* (Minneapolis: Augsburg, 1990), pp. 35-36.

2. Donald Juel, *A Master of Surprise* (Minneapolis: Fortress Press, 1994), p. 36.

3. *Ibid.*, p. 40.

Mark 1:9-15

We will begin commentary here with v. 12 where we hear that the Spirit drove Jesus out into the wilderness to be tempted by Satan for forty days. The nature of the temptation is omitted. Both Matthew and Luke tell this story in much richer detail. Old Testament analogies immediately come to mind. The number forty in *days* is reminiscent of the forty *years* that Israel spent in the wilderness. According to Jeremiah 2:1-3 the wilderness was a time of youthful devotion on behalf of Israel. During this time the Moses-led people were fed with manna from on high. In Ezekiel 20:9-26, however, the wilderness experience is understood as a time of Israel's rebellion. Many passages in the Psalms also picture Israel in the wilderness as a time when Israel failed the test of obedience. It may be, therefore, that Mark presents Jesus as the head of a New Israel who is driven into the wilderness and remains obedient to the testing of God.

Besides Moses the other Old Testament figure who spent time (forty days and nights) in the wilderness was the prophet Elijah (1 Kings 19:1-18). It may be that Mark intends to call both Moses and Elijah to remembrance in these verses. It will be Moses and Elijah who are present with Jesus on the mountain of transfiguration (Mark 9:2-8). Allusions to Moses and Elijah accompany the voice from heaven which names Jesus "Son of God." (See 1:11 and 9:7.)

Jesus' encounter with Satan in the wilderness is probably related to the baptismal scene. In the baptismal scene we hear clearly who Jesus is. He is the Son of God. In the wilderness is revealed to us a major task of the Son of God. He will overthrow the rule of Satan and bring in the fulfilled time of salvation. Defeat of the evil powers is a central objective of Jesus' ministry. When Jesus appointed the twelve to be with him he sent them out to preach the good news of the kingdom (the positive side of the message) and to cast out demons (the negative side of the message) (Mark 3:13-15).

John is arrested in 1:14. Mark strikes his first ominous note early on! The mission of John and Jesus in the world will be met with deadly opposition.

Galilee is the geographical setting for the first part of Mark's Gospel. Jesus of Nazareth, the Son of God, begins his ministry in Galilee. Jesus comes into Galilee preaching! He preaches in the fulfillment of time. "The time is fulfilled, and the kingdom of God has come near; repent, and believe in the good news" (1:15). These are the first words Jesus speaks in this Gospel. First words are not chosen by accident! The program of the Son of God is laid out before us. The Son will bring the kingdom of God to earth. Final matters are of importance here.

One of the ways that the Son of God will bring in the kingdom is through preaching. Jack Dean Kingsbury notes that this passage which presents Jesus as a preacher is the beginning of a series of passages which summarize for us the nature of Jesus' ministry in Galilee.

> ... he will preach (1:14-15), call disciples (1:16-20), teach (1:21-22), and heal and exorcize demons (1:32-34). And to make certain that the reader does not lose sight of the fact that it is just such activity that occupies Jesus during this phase of his ministry, Mark dots the pages of 1:14— 8:26 with additional summary-passages: Jesus continues to preach (1:38-39), to call disciples (2:14; 3:13-19), to teach (2:13; 6:6b, 30-34; cf. 4:1-2; 10:1), and to heal and to exorcize demons (1:39; 3:7-12; 6:53-56).[1]

The structure of Mark is such that after the baptism Jesus immediately begins his ministry. Kingsbury is helpful in showing us how the appearance of these stories of Jesus in action is symbolic of the whole ministry of Jesus. Once we have moved through Mark 1 we have heard the nature of Jesus' ministry as Son of God. He is the one who preaches, calls disciples, teaches and heals and exorcizes evil spirits. Preaching may be the most important activity of this ministry as it tends to bind these activities together.

Mark introduces the theme of repentance and faith as the response that is called forth by Jesus' preaching. Jesus calls humanity to a time of listening, a time of decision. It is time to turn our lives around and believe the good news announced by Jesus that the kingdom of God has come near to us. Faith tends to be the possession of "the little people" in Mark's Gospel. Jesus saw the faith of the men who brought a paralytic for healing: 2:5. The woman with the flow of blood is healed because Jesus saw her faith: 5:34. Bartimaeus moved from blindness to sight because of his faith: 10:52. Jesus' disciples, on the other hand, have more fear than faith. On a stormy night Jesus calmed a storm and brought safety to the disciples. "Why are you afraid?" he asked the disciples. "Have you still no faith?" (Mark 4:35-41). Faith and unfaith turn up in interesting places in this surprising Gospel.

Homiletical Directions

A first possibility with this brief text would be to create a sermon around the *wilderness* motif. Tell aspects of the stories of Moses and Elijah in the wilderness. These were times of testing, but God brought them through the testing time. Next tell the story of the Son of God who is driven into the wilderness. God is with him as he, too, withstands the test. The good news in this bracket of stories is that there is help and comfort for us when our lives land in the wilderness testing-time. The living center of proclamation for such stories might go something like this: "I walked with Moses and the Israelites through the wilderness for forty years. I brought them to the land of promise. I walked with Elijah for forty days and nights in the wilderness on the way to Mount Horeb. I called him to new purposes in life. I walked with my beloved Son as he encountered Satan in the wilderness. I raised him up from even the darkest hour. I will walk with you through the wilderness as well. I have a land of promise for you. I have a mission for you to accomplish. I will raise you from every darkness."

The brief verse that sets forth Jesus' mission among us is not in story form. Jesus simply announces that "The time is fulfilled, and the kingdom of God has come near; repent, and believe in the good news." Herein lies the program of Mark's Gospel. The Son of God has come to call people to repentance and faith. And how shall it go? We have made reference to "the little people" in Mark's story who do believe the good news. [See the above discussion on Mark 2:1-2 (v. 5); 5:24-34 (v. 34) and 10:46-52 (v. 52).] Each of these stories can be told as stories of those who hear the good news and believe. They have heard Jesus say, "... repent, and believe in the good news," and they have believed what they have heard.

This living center of proclamation spoken by Jesus Christ is also addressed to us today. Jesus says to us, "The time is fulfilled, and the kingdom of God has come near; repent, and believe in the good news." "Let anyone with ears to hear listen!" (Mark 4:9). Mark's whole Gospel is a plea to us to hear and believe, to see and understand!

Another possibility is to make use of the Parable of the Sower if you have not already done so. (See the notes on this parable in the Introduction and in chapter 12.) Many people suggest that the Parable of the Sower is the plot summary of the first part of Mark's Gospel. Jesus has come preaching. The time is fulfilled. People are to repent and believe. But the soil of human hearts is not always ready to receive the blessings of the One Who Sows. We can tell of the variety of soils and their response to the Sower. *Be careful* in following this suggestion, however, that the message is not simply a kind of *imperative that demands of people that they be good soil.* The good news is not that we can make ourselves good soil. The good news is that the Sower keeps on sowing with generous liberality until the hardened soil of our hearts repents and comes to faith.

"I am a generous sower," Jesus says. "I will sow and sow and sow until my seed cracks open the soil of your heart. I will sow until the soil of your heart bears fruit, thirtyfold, sixtyfold and hundredfold."

Still another preaching possibility would be to follow up Kingsbury's point that preaching, calling disciples, teaching and healing and exorcism are the aspects of Jesus' ministry as he brings near the kingdom. Stories of Jesus engaged in each of these aspects of ministry could be told as a way of communicating what it means that Jesus brings near the kingdom. After each of these stories the

41

theme verse from Mark 1:15 could be repeated. The sermon would end with this proclamation ringing in people's ears: "The time is fulfilled, and the kingdom of God has come near; repent, and believe in the good news."

---

1. Jack Dean Kingsbury, *The Christology of Mark's Gospel* (Philadelphia: Fortress Press, 1983), p. 72.

Mark 1:14-20

The first two verses of this pericope have been commented on in chapter 3. The action here is in Galilee. In v. 16 Jesus calls his first disciples as he passes along the Sea of Galilee. There are several references to the Sea of Galilee in these early chapters of Mark: 2:13; 3:7; 4:1. Tolbert believes that these locational references would have indicated the presence of a division of thought for the first hearers of the Gospel.[1]

In her way of structuring the Gospel, Tolbert outlines the material from 1:16—3:6 with special reference to Jesus' call of the disciples. Following the call of Simon and Andrew, James and John in this pericope, there are *four healing stories*. Following the call of Levi, the son of Alphaeus, in 2:13-14, there are *four controversy stories*. The Pharisees are party to these controversies. Remember, too, Kingsbury's point that the pericopes in Mark 1 set forth the four aspects of Jesus' ministry: preaching, calling disciples, teaching and healing and exorcism. Following either Tolbert or Kingsbury we see that this initial calling of disciples is part of a larger story in Mark's Gospel. This is not an isolated pericope! This text has intertextual connections with other material in Mark's Gospel.

An important reality about today's text is the manner in which Jesus calls his disciples. The initiative in calling disciples here, as always, is solely in Jesus' hands. People don't volunteer for discipleship. They are invited. They are called. Jesus graciously invited Peter and Simon, and James and John to *follow*. The initiating grace of Jesus' call to discipleship should mark the way we talk about that call in the context of the Gospels or in our contemporary context.

Simon and Andrew are the first disciples to be called. Simon! Those of us who know this story know that things will not turn out so well for Simon. He has his high moments. Jesus gives him the surname: Peter/Rock (Mark 3:15). It was Simon who gave reply for the disciples when Jesus asked them, "But who do you say that I am?" Simon answered: "You are the Messiah" (Mark 8:29-30). In the days of Jesus' passion, however, Simon denied his Lord. "I do not know or understand what you are talking about," Peter said to the question of the servant-girls (Mark 14:68). Three times Peter denied his Lord. And yet in the story of the first Easter the angel commands the women to tell Peter that Jesus has gone before them into Galilee (Mark 16:7). There is hope for Peter. There is hope for us, as well, even after we have been faithless disciples.

This introduction of the theme of failure on the part of Peter raises the larger issue of the failure of the disciples in general in Mark's telling of the story. These failures seem to come in *threes*. Peter denied his Lord three times. There are three boat scenes in Mark's Gospel where Jesus encounters the disciples. (See Mark 4:35-41; 6:45-51; 8:14-21.) Each scene etches a sense of failure on the part of the disciples. They are afraid. They don't understand who Jesus is when he calms the storm. "Who then is this, that even the wind and the sea obey him?" They were astounded at his walking on the sea. When they saw him come walking to them on the sea they were terrified. Mark tells us that "... they were utterly astounded, for they did not understand about the loaves, but their hearts were hardened" (Mark 6:52). When we reach the third boat scene Jesus is indignant with his disciples. "Do you still not perceive or understand? Are your hearts hardened? Do you have eyes, and fail to see? Do you have ears, and fail to hear?" (Mark 8:17-18).

There is another set of three scenes centered in Jesus' revealing to the disciples that "... the Son of Man must undergo great suffering ..." (Mark 8:31-38; 9:30-37; 10:32-45). In each of these scenes Jesus reveals to the disciples that he must endure the cross. In each case they refuse to think of the cross. They are too busy thinking of glory, their own glory! (See chapter 21.)

There is much evidence to support Tolbert's hypothesis that the disciples are the kind of hearers of the word of Jesus who are rocky ground. Remember the surname Jesus gave to Peter! He called him "rock." "And these are the ones sown on *rocky* ground: when they hear the word, they immediately receive it with joy. But they have no root, and endure only for a while; then, when trouble or persecution arises on account of the word, immediately they fall away" (Mark 4:6-17).

Homiletical Directions

The call of the disciples introduces us to a handful of followers of Jesus whom Mark will track for us throughout the Gospel. We could certainly tell some of those "stories of three" in this week's sermon. On the other hand, it might be a bit premature to lay bare the not so pretty tale of the twelve. We can tell these stories later after we have heard a bit more about these chosen ones.

This text is appointed in the Epiphany Season of the Church's year. Mission is a dominant theme of this season of the Church's life. The text before us supplies us with a call to mission. "Follow me and I will make you fish for people" (Mark 1:17). One of the ways of putting stories together in sermonic form is by *alternation*. Alternatively we tell the Bible's story and make appropriate comments, tell another Bible story and make a comment, and so on. We alternate between telling the stories of the Bible and commenting on these stories for our lives today. The story gives structure to our sermon. At points along the way we offer a teaching commentary on the story.

One possible way to do this is to follow the story of Peter through Mark's Gospel. Story One would simply tell of the call of Peter to follow as we have it in our text today. Our comment on this story might be to note that it is not only Peter and Andrew, James and John who are called to follow Jesus. We are called to follow Jesus in our day as well. The gracious invitation falls upon our ears. Our comment on this first story might simply be to make sure that each one who hears our sermon hears Jesus' words as their call to mission. Each hearer is confronted by the words of Jesus: "Follow me and I will make you fish for people."

We alternate now and go back to the story of Peter. In Mark 6:7-13 Jesus sends Peter and the disciples on a "fishing" expedition. Jesus sent the disciples into mission. In so doing he gave them authority over unclean spirits. The disciples preached so that their

45

listeners repented; they healed the sick with the anointing of oil. We don't hear anything specific about Peter here, but we assume he is being shaped by his call and his discipleship. In Mark 8:27-30 when Jesus asks the disciples who they think he is, Peter makes his confession. "You are the Messiah," Peter proclaims.

Our comment on this second story of Peter can indicate the kinds of mission Jesus has in mind when he calls us to follow. Jesus calls. He also sends! We can lay out for our hearers an understanding of what it means to follow Jesus today.

Alternating back to the story of Peter, we tell a third story, the story of Peter's denial (Mark 14:53-72). Our comment on this story might be a reminder of our many failures in mission. The way Mark tells the story, following and failing seem to go hand in hand. That's just as true today as it was in the day of Mark.

As a final story we can tell the Easter text with a focus on the role of Peter (Mark 16:1-8). The last we heard from Peter was that he denied his Lord three times just as Jesus had predicted. But Peter's failure is not to be the last word! There is still hope for Peter. There is still hope for us. "... go tell his disciples and Peter that he is going ahead of you to Galilee; there you will see him, just as he told you" (Mark 16:7). Our final comment on these stories of Peter is a hopeful word! Jesus' call to mission has not ended with our failures. In the light of Easter the power of new life is released into our very bodies in order that we might be empowered by the One who has called us to faithful following. Easter is the power of mission!

----

1. Mary Ann Tolbert, *Sowing The Gospel* (Minneapolis: Fortress Press, 1989), p. 131.

Mark 1:21-28

The story of the man in the synagogue with an unclean spirit fits structures in Mark which have been discussed earlier. Jack Dean Kingsbury sees this as one of the series of events in this chapter which characterize Jesus as One who comes preaching, calling disciples, teaching, and healing and exorcizing demons. Mary Ann Tolbert sees this story as one of a series of four healing stories followed by four controversy stories which inaugurate Jesus' ministry. In either way of looking at this story we are invited to see it as part of a larger pattern of stories.

This opening act of Jesus' ministry is set in a holy place on a holy day: in the synagogue on the sabbath. The One who is to bring the kingdom comes immediately into conflict with the powers that work against kingdom life. Jesus confronts these powers head-on. With authority he casts out the unclean spirit. Juel refers to Jesus' action as a "foretaste of the feast to come." In this story Jesus begins his assault on those forces arrayed against the kingdom of God. Jesus is engaged in an eschatological conflict with Satan. Later, when Jesus appoints the twelve, he appoints them into a ministry of engagement with the powers. "And he appointed twelve ... to be sent out to proclaim the message *and to have authority to cast out demons*" (Mark 3:14-15). Kingsbury refers to such remarkable deeds of Jesus' power as "... naked revelations of his divine sonship and the circumstance that in him God's Rule is a present reality."[1]

The confession of the man with the unclean spirit that he knows who Jesus is gives this story great importance in the Gospel narrative. The only other person who seems to get it right is the centurion at the cross in 15:39. The disciples never get it right! Peter appears to have it right in 8:27-30 when he identifies Jesus as the Messiah. Only two verses later, however, Peter rebukes Jesus' talk of the cross and suffering. Jesus then rebukes Peter. "Get behind me Satan! For you are setting your mind not on divine things but on human things" (Mark 8:33). Mark's story tells so often of those who fail to see and perceive, to hear and understand. The man with the unclean spirit in the *beginning* and the centurion at the cross at the *ending* get it right. When Mark tells the story in this way he invites us to consider *our response* to the authoritative presence of Jesus Christ.

The reality of the silence concerning the true identity of Jesus first appears in this passage. When the unclean spirit identifies Jesus as the "Holy One of God" Jesus rebukes him and calls for silence! (1:25). Peter's confession is initially met with silence as well: "And he [Jesus] sternly ordered them not to tell anyone about him" (Mark 8:30). Much has been written about this silence motif in Mark's Gospel. What is the purpose of this Messianic Secret? Perhaps it is simply a way for Mark to keep our eyes open and our ears alert in our own response to the One who teaches with authority.

This One who teaches with authority, and not as the scribes, demonstrates his authority through the power of his spoken word. Scribal authority was based on their ability to recite the opinion of many Rabbis on a given topic. Jesus' word had authority because when he spoke, it came to pass. "Come out of him," Jesus commanded of the unclean spirit. "And the unclean spirit, convulsing him and crying with a loud voice, came out of him" (Mark 1:26). We will hear Jesus speak this authoritative word many times in Mark's Gospel. (See Mark 1:41; 2:5, 11, 14.) This power of the word calls to mind God's creation of the world as told in Genesis 1. God spoke, and it was so! "God said, 'Let there be light'; and there was light" (Genesis 1:3). God spoke the creation into being. That is most certainly an authoritative word!

God also spoke words of promise that came to pass. God spoke a word of promise to Abraham and Sarah in Genesis 12:1-3. "I will make of you a great nation, and I will bless you, and make your name great, so that you will be a blessing" (Genesis 12:2). In the book of Joshua we hear that God's promises were fulfilled. "... Not one thing has failed of all the good things that the Lord your God promised concerning you; all have come to pass for you, not one of them has failed" (Joshua 23:14).

God spoke a word of promise to David that became the foundation of all Messianic hopes. "When your days [David] are fulfilled and you lie down with your ancestors, I will raise up your offspring after you, who shall come forth from your body, and I will establish his kingdom. He shall build a house for my name, and I will establish the throne of his kingdom forever" (2 Samuel 7:12-13).

God also spoke words of promise through the prophets. Through the mouth of the prophet Isaiah we hear the Bible's clearest teaching on the authoritative word of God:

> *For as the rain and the snow come down from heaven*
> *and do not return there until*
> *they have watered the earth,*
> *making it bring forth and sprout,*
> *giving seed to the sower and bread to the eater,*
> ***so shall my word be that goes out from my mouth;***
> *it shall not return to me empty,*
> *but it shall accomplish that which I purpose,*
> *and succeed in the thing for which I sent it.*
>
> (Isaiah 55:10-11)

In the New Testament we hear that "the word became flesh and lived among us" (John 1:14). This word-made-flesh speaks, and it is so! He commands the demons and they come out. He forgives sin and it is forgiven. He speaks a word of healing and healing is accomplished. "What is this? A new teaching — with authority! He commands even the unclean spirits, and they obey him" (1:27).

Homiletical Directions

We remember Kingsbury's point that Jesus' ministry has four aspects in Mark's Gospel: preaching, teaching, calling disciples, and healing and exorcism. This story could, therefore, be told as one of this series of four realities in the ministry of Jesus. The problem with this approach will be that each of these four consecutive texts in Mark 1 are part of the Cycle B Lectionary.

49

However we may choose to group them together we must also deal with each text in its particularity during the course of these weeks.

Another approach to preaching on this text would be to focus on the *confession* of the man with an unclean spirit that Jesus is the Holy One of God. This story could be coupled with the story of Peter's confession and the confession of the centurion. The reality of our own confessional status in relationship to this One with authority is brought into focus through these stories.

A third approach to this text might be to focus on the reality that Jesus brings the kingdom of God by confronting the powers of evil with an authoritative word of God. Story One can retell the text with a focus on the authoritative word: "Be silent, and come out of him!" Jesus hurls a word at all those forces which would stand in the way of the coming of God's kingdom, and his word triumphs. A little word overthrows them!

Story Two can be a journey through the Hebrew Bible as we catch the full meaning of God's creative word. One of the ways that God creates the world is through the power of an authoritative word: Genesis 1. The stories of God's promissory word to Abraham and David are further expositions of the power of God's promise. The passage from Isaiah 55 and John 1 might also be referred to as we seek to explicate for our listeners the nature of the Word of God in Scripture. These stories from Scripture help us get a clearer image of what Jesus is doing when he says: "Be silent, and come out of him!" It might be that these stories should precede rather than follow the retelling of the text for the day.

Story Three might well center in bondage stories of our time. Mark's Gospel centers in the reality that "... the time is fulfilled, and the kingdom of God has come near; repent, and believe in the good news" (Mark 1:15). When the kingdom of God comes near, God is at work. God's son pushes back the powers that impede life. Unclean spirits are precisely such forces. Yet these are forces which threaten our lives today. You will have your own ways of describing the ways these forces impact human lives today. It can certainly be done by telling some contemporary stories of lives in the grasp of forces that attack life.

The good news is that the Jesus, who encountered the man with an unclean spirit long ago with an authoritative word, is alive today speaking such words to today's bound people. The heart of the sermon might well be for today's hearers to hear Jesus' word as a word addressed to them as they live their lives in the midst of life-threatening forces. "Jesus' word for you today," we say, "is, 'Be silent, and come out!' " We can enumerate the kinds of bondage that people experience. We say, "Many of us today are afflicted with the unclean spirit of despair in the face of the forces that seek to overwhelm us. But there is good news! Jesus says to those forces today, 'Be silent, and come out!' " Enumerate the names of the forces. Follow each enumeration with the simple word of authority: "Be silent, and come out!" This is gospel *proclamation*!

---

1. Jack Dean Kingsbury, *The Christology of Mark's Gospel* (Philadelphia: Fortress Press, 1983), p. 77.

Mark 1:29-39

We note again that this passage is one of four healing stories which inaugurate Jesus' ministry. Healing and exorcism play a role in Mark's Gospel that is far greater than either our customary summarizing of the themes of Mark's Gospel or our theologizing about the nature of Jesus' ministry. Healing and exorcism stories do not translate well into our modern or postmodern world. Rudolf Bultmann once tried to rid the Bible of these stories once and for all with his program of demythologizing. The fact is, however, that people do still get sick. The fact is that our lives are thwarted by powers and forces over which we seem to have no control. Let us, therefore, not let these stories die a premature death! There is probably more power in the simple re-telling of these stories than we can rationally realize!

Jesus' first healing in Capernaum (1:21-28) was the healing of a *man* with an unclean spirit. The first of the stories in this pericope is the healing of a *woman*, Simon's mother-in-law. This pattern replays itself in Mark 5 when Jesus goes to the other side of the sea into the country of the Gerasenes. Mark 5 relays the story of the healing of a *man* possessed by an unclean spirit followed by stories of the healing of a *woman* with a flow of blood and a *girl* who was at the point of death. This coupling of stories about men and women seems to be an intentional pattern in Mark.

Many healings are reported in these verses. We ought to remember that in the world view of Jesus' time illness was thought to be caused by some form of evil or evil spirit. Healing poses no problem for Jesus as yet. When he heals in the synagogue on the sabbath, however, plots to destroy him arise (Mark 3:1-6).

The theme of *silence* arises again in v. 34. Jesus would not permit those who know him, the demons, to speak about him. (See also 3:12.) Those who know Jesus are not allowed to speak. Others are not intended to know until his journey comes to an end. Jesus does finally begin to teach the disciples who he is. In Mark 8:31-32; 9:30-31; and 10:32-34 Jesus reveals to the disciples that his identity is bound up with his sufferings, passion and death at the hands of the chief priests and scribes. When the suffering is complete, when he has been buried in the tomb, then, after three days, he will rise again. Only then, at the end of the journey, will his full identity be known.

In Mark's telling of the story, therefore, it is only at the end that people will *know* who Jesus really is. The unnamed woman at Simon's house in Bethany seems to know! She pours an alabaster jar of ointment over his head. Jesus interprets her action as anointing for his burial. This wonderful and important story of the unnamed woman is omitted in the lectionary cycle. It only appears on the Sunday of the Passion as part of the lengthy text: Mark 14:1—15:47.

So a *woman* knows who Jesus is. So does a *man*, an unlikely man, a Roman Centurion: 15:39. Mark turns expectations upside down with these stories of those who know. The disciples surely don't know. The women at the tomb flee in fear. But there is a woman with no name and a Roman Centurion who penetrate the mystery and bear witness for us. Strange models of faith these! One never knows just where faith is liable to burst into bloom. It would be important at some point in the Markan year to tell the stories of this woman and this man as paradigms of the faithful. There might be great comfort for our common folk in hearing of the very common ones who seem to be the first to know!

In 1:35-38 we have the first dispute between Jesus and his disciples. They have different agendas. The disciples want Jesus to return to yesterday's crowd. Jesus protests. He is on a journey, a journey the disciples cannot comprehend. He wills to move on to the next towns; his eye is on the future. We get a preview here of the disputes and misunderstandings between Jesus and his disciples that are present throughout Mark's Gospel.

Jesus does head for new towns throughout Galilee where he preaches and casts out demons. We come again to the matter of exorcism. Exorcisms are mentioned three times in Mark 1. (See

Mark 1:25, 34, 39.) This topic recurs regularly throughout Mark's story. Jesus empowers his disciples to join him in the ministry of exorcism: 3:15; 6:7, 13. As indicated earlier, this ministry of Jesus in relation to demons is most assuredly part of the battle being waged by the in-breaking reign of God (which Jesus has announced, 1:15) and the principalities and powers of the present darkness.

In a story told in Mark 3:20-30 the scribes from Jerusalem challenge Jesus' authority to cast out demons. They are clearly aware that if Jesus has such power it would be a sign of his divine origin. They argue, therefore, that "... He has Beelzebul, and by the ruler of the demons he casts out demons" (Mark 3:22). The Jerusalem scribes deem it important to challenge Jesus on this point. Everyone knows what is at stake here! The source of Jesus' authority and identity is at stake. Jesus defends his authority over evil spirits. "How can Satan cast out Satan?" he asks. "If a kingdom is divided against itself, that kingdom cannot stand" (Mark 3:23-24). This story is appointed for the Fourth Sunday of Pentecost.

In chapter 5:1-20 a story is told about a Gerasene demoniac. This story is not in the Markan lectionary cycle. Mark 7:24-30 tells of Jesus' encounter with a Greek woman, a Syrophoenician, whose daughter was possessed by an unclean spirit. This story is designated for the Seventeenth Sunday of Pentecost. It is the only story in Mark's Gospel where Jesus gets a theology lesson! The upshot of the story is that Jesus' power over unclean spirits is a power meant for Jews *and Gentiles* alike.

In Mark 9:14-29, a story not in the lectionary, Jesus casts out a dumb spirit. His "faithless disciples" had tried to exorcise this demon but they could not. The father of the boy with the dumb spirit takes his case to Jesus, saying, " '... if you are able to do anything, have pity on us and help us.' Jesus said to him, 'If you are able! — All things can be done for the one who believes.' Immediately the father of the child cried out, 'I believe; help my unbelief' " (Mark 9:22-24). Jesus spoke a word (!) and the boy was healed.

In Mark 9:28-31 we hear the disciples complain to Jesus that they saw a man, obviously a man they did not know, casting out a demon in Jesus' name. The disciples forbade the man to continue his practice but Jesus said, "Do not stop him, for no one who does a deed of power in my name will be able soon afterward to speak evil of me" (Mark 9:39). This story appears in the lectionary on the Twentieth Sunday of Pentecost.

One more story of Jesus and the powers of darkness might be that part of the story of his crucifixion where we hear that the sky turned black at midday (Mark 15:33). Is this Satan's last burst of darkness? Is this a symbol of Jesus' struggle with the Ruler of Darkness? Will the Son of God, who promised to bring God's reign of light and life, be snuffed out in darkness and death? We must turn to the story of Easter dawn in the next chapter, Mark 16:1-8, to discover that the light has truly shined in the darkness! The powers of darkness have been vanquished once and for all!

Homiletical Directions

In Mark's story it is the demons who seem to know who Jesus is. They are commanded to be silent. We would expect that the disciples would be those who know. They are silent except for Peter's confession which is quickly followed by a rebuke of Jesus (Mark 8:29, 33). There is a strange irony here that is further compounded by the fact that it is an unnamed woman and a Roman Centurion who do know Jesus' identity. This aspect of Mark's story ought to be addressed sometime during this Church Year. These stories could well be told in a way that would lead to the question of *our* knowing.

The stories in the first chapter of Mark display in a rather dramatic way the entrance of the One who has ripped open the heavens to dwell among us. "The time is fulfilled," Jesus says. "The kingdom of God has come near." Jesus then proceeds to engage in a series of acts of ministry, the center of which appears to be his exorcising activity. The kingdom of God comes and a battle with demons is engaged! This might be a good place in the lectionary year to bring these stories to light. Story One can tell the stories in this pericope with a glance back at last week's pericope to focus attention on the divine encounter with evil.

Stories Two and Three could be those other stories in the Gospel of Mark which are *not* in the Cycle B lectionary and which carry out this theme of Jesus' engagement with the powers. Mark 5:1-20 is the story of the Gerasene demoniac. At the heart of this story stands Jesus' word of proclamation: "Come out of the man, you unclean spirit!" Tell this story in a way that features Jesus' word as a climax.

Mark 9:14-29 is the other story of Jesus' engagement with the powers that is not in the Cycle B lectionary. Again the story could be told in such a way that Jesus' proclamatory word is the focus: "You spirit that keeps this boy from speaking and hearing, I command you, come out of him, and never enter him again!"

Story Four would move to the darkness at high noon on the day of Jesus' crucifixion: Mark 15:33-34. Jesus cries out in the midst of the darkness, wondering aloud if God, too, has forsaken him. The question becomes acute. Is this the time of fulfillment? Has the Kingdom of God really come near? Or has something gone terribly wrong?

The Easter story in Mark 16 is needed to enlighten this darkness. "He has been raised; he is not here. Look, there is the place they laid him" (Mark 16:6). The author of the book of Colossians summarizes the meaning of the Jesus story in relation to the powers of evil in these words: "He disarmed the rulers and authorities and made a public example of them, triumphing over them in it" (Colossians 2:15). This can be turned into first person, present tense language as a climax of this sermon. The Jesus of these Markan stories finally says to us:

"I have disarmed the rulers and authorities of this time and place."

"I have made a public example of the powers of darkness."

"I have triumphed over all the forces of the night which seek to hold your lives in darkness."

"The time is fulfilled. I have brought the kingdom near for you. Live boldly in the light of Easter's new day." Amen.

Mark 1:40-45

We have before us this week another healing story as the One who brings God's reign explodes into ministry with God's life-giving power! This time it is an unclean leper who *comes to Jesus.* This has been characteristic of the healings and exorcisms in Mark's first chapter: people come to Jesus for help. One wonders at times if this is Mark's story-formed way of telling us what faith is. Faith is people in deep need who come to Jesus in their desperation! In the case of the leper we could add to this definition. The leper comes *believing* that Jesus does, indeed, have authority over leprosy. (Remember the discussion concerning Jesus' authority in the story told in Mark 1:21-28, see v. 27.) "If you choose," the leper says to Jesus, "you can make me clean." A man in need comes to Jesus, trusting that Jesus has the authority in his word to make him clean. Such is Mark's picture of a faithful one.

Jesus responds to a leper in need. "I do choose," Jesus says. "Be made clean!" Immediately the leprosy left him and he was clean. We have yet another instance here of the power and authority of Jesus' word. His word is not like the words and the authority of the scribes. His word has the power to do what it says. God's creative word has become flesh in this man Jesus. When Jesus speaks, God performs. The leper's faith has a new reality to deal with. The word of Jesus has made him clean. As Saint Paul puts it: "... faith comes from what is heard, and what is heard comes through the word of Christ" (Romans 10:17).

A full New Testament picture of faith will always include the reality that faith is called into being by the creative, authoritative word of Jesus Christ. *Faith is coming to Jesus in the midst of our desperate need.* If that is the only dimension of faith, however, then faith is a human creation. *Faith is called forth from us in its fullness by the word that Jesus speaks to us.* Again, if we were only to emphasize the divine word that calls faith into being we would be in danger of making robots of the faithful. Faith emerges from the intersection where Jesus with his word meets us with our desperate need. How spirit-driven faith arises from this intersection is a mystery. Whatever we say about faith beyond the reality of the work of the Spirit at the intersection of human need and Christ's word will probably lead us into some form of heresy!

There is an important caution to preachers at this point. Preaching, after all, takes place precisely at this divine/human intersection. We speak God's word which creates new realities and calls people to faith. We need to be very careful here about our *job descriptions*. It is our job at this intersection to speak Christ's word with authority in our preaching. It is the Spirit's job to take that word on the long, long journey from human ear to human heart. The story is told that Martin Luther was once chastised for drinking beer in a Wittenberg pub. "How can the reformation move forward while you sit here drinking beer?" someone asked him. "The Holy Spirit will take care of the reformation," Luther is said to have replied. Luther knew how to keep his job and the Spirit's job separate from each other. If creating faith in human hearts were *our* job, wouldn't every preacher die of a panic of overwork!

Jesus sends the cleansed leper to a priest to offer for cleansing as Moses had commanded. Leviticus 14 spells out the duties of priests in relation to leprosy. (If you have never told the story of the priestly task in relation to leprosy as outlined in the Hebrew Bible, this might be a good time to do so.) It was the priest's task to pronounce the leper "Clean" or "Unclean." It is worthwhile noting that it is the uncleanness occasioned by the leprosy that is the central issue and not the disease itself. We should note as well that Jesus at this point is not ready to put the priests and the temple out of business. That day will come!

The man who was made clean spoke freely of the powerful word of Jesus that had bathed his body with health. People flocked to Jesus in reaction to this man's testimony. So many people came to find Jesus, in fact, that he could no longer enter their towns. Is that why Jesus ordered so many of those whom he healed to keep silent?

Donald Juel has an important treatment of this story in his Markan commentary. He points out that this story is the first of several stories that deal with Jesus' violation of *ritual boundaries.* In chapter 2 reference was made to Juel's organizing insight concerning the tearing of the heavens.[1] Juel sees Mark's Jesus as the One who tears open the heavens and transcends the boundaries between heaven and earth in order to be loose in this world. He characterizes parts of Jesus' ministry as transcending or transgressing boundaries. Boundaries had been established in Israel for the protection of the community. Boundaries helped Israel maintain her identity. And then Jesus comes along transgressing the boundaries and offering people a new identity. In the stories that follow Jesus transgresses the boundary of God's prerogative to forgive sin as he himself proclaims forgiveness (Mark 2:1-12). Jesus proceeds to eat with the unwashed (Mark 2:15-17), eat the bread of the Presence (Mark 2:23-28), and heal on the Sabbath (Mark 3:1-6).

Jesus refuses to recognize the religious boundaries of his day! He tears apart old ways of being religious and old ways of maintaining identity. A person in need is simply more important than religiously defined boundaries. A new way of God's relating to humans is at loose in the world. A new way of relating to God, the way of faith, becomes an open possibility.

Homiletical Directions

We could identify *faith* as the focal point of a sermon on this text. Enough has been said in the comments above on the matter of faith to give some theological substance to a sermon on faith. It is probably premature, however, to tackle the topic of "faith" in Mark's Gospel. Mark still has much to say on the reality of faith. A key passage will be Mark 4:35-41. Jesus is asleep in the boat with his disciples. A great storm arises on the sea and Jesus sleeps on! The disciples wake Jesus and cry out for his help. Jesus' response to their frantic behavior is surprising. "Why are you afraid?" he asks them. "Have you still no faith?" Two responses to Jesus are presented in this story. People can be *in fear* in Jesus' presence or they can have *faith*. The contrast between fear and faith will be a strong theme in later chapters of this Gospel.

We have identified a series of passages in Mark 1:40—3:6 where Jesus transgresses the religious boundaries of his day. Each of these texts will occur in the Cycle B lectionary. Still, it might be well at some point to treat these passages together so that the reality of Jesus' boundary-breaking will be seen in its fullness. Since today's text is the first such story in this list, now is as good a time as ever to treat these stories holistically. This means that the stories we will tell this week are the stories of transgressing boundaries: Mark 1:40-45; Mark 2:1-12; Mark 2:15-17; Mark 2:23-28 and Mark 3:1-6. Each story needs to be briefly told. The two stories of the Sabbath, Mark 2:23-28 and 3:1-6, might best be told together.

The thread that holds our stories together could be the theme of transgressing or breaking boundaries. Jesus breaks down old ways of thinking about one's relationship to God. Jesus offers a new way to understand our identity as God's people. Our identity is not as clean or unclean people. "Be made clean!" Jesus says to us (Mark 1:41). "I give you a new identity as sons and daughters of God's word."

Our identity is no longer that of sinner. "Your sins are forgiven," Jesus says to us (Mark 2:5). "I give you a new identity as sons and daughters of God's word."

Our identity as righteous ones is no longer achieved by eating with the right people, people who wash their hands in the right way. "I have come to call not the righteous but sinners," Jesus says (Mark 2:17). "I give you a new identity as sons and daughters of God's word."

Our identity is no longer secured through sabbath-keeping wherein keeping the sabbath law is more important than people. "The Sabbath was made for humankind, and not humankind for the Sabbath," Jesus says (Mark 2:27). "I give you a new identity as sons and daughters of God's word."

You may further wish to pursue ways in which people in your context set up boundaries that they use to identify themselves as God's people. Jesus Christ wishes to break down all such boundaries. A colleague of mine once cautioned about drawing such boundaries. "Be careful when you draw lines," he would say. "Whenever you draw a line (boundary) which helps to tell you who is in and who is out of God's people — remember — Jesus is always on the other side of the line!"

---

1. Donald H. Juel, *Mark* (Minneapolis: Augsburg, 1990), pp. 43-45.

Mark 2:1-12

This week's pericope is interconnected with many Markan stories and themes. It is the fourth in the series of healing stories that we have been dealing with in recent weeks. On the other hand, it is the first in a series of *controversy* stories that now occur. Controversy stories have some regular features. A question is usually asked of Jesus which seems to be a critique of his ministry in the light of Jewish tradition. The four questions in this series are: "Why does this fellow speak in this way? It is blasphemy! Who can forgive sins but God alone?" (Mark 2:7). "Why does he eat with tax collectors and sinners?" (Mark 2:16). "Why do John's disciples and the disciples of the Pharisees fast, but your disciples do not fast?" (Mark 2:18). "Look, why are they doing what is not lawful on the Sabbath?" (Mark 2:24). Jesus' reply in each case is a *pronouncement* of some kind that settles the matter.

Controversy now arises in the ministry of Jesus. Mary Ann Tolbert points out that the stories in Mark 1:16 — 2:12 are a kind of parallel with the stories in 2:13 — 3:6.[1] Each of these segments begins with the calling of disciples (1:16-20; 2:13-14). The general tenor of the stories in 1:16ff. is *positive*. People accept Jesus and his mighty words and deeds. This segment ends with the glad announcement: "We have never seen anything like this!" (Mark 2:12).

The general tenor of the stories which begin in 2:13, on the other hand, is *negative* in tone. People reject Jesus. This series of stories ends with the ominous words: "The Pharisees went out and immediately conspired with the Herodians against him, how to destroy him" (Mark 3:6). In our text for today, for example, the Pharisees accuse Jesus of blasphemy. "No one can forgive sins save God alone," they protest. In Jesus' trial at the end of Mark's Gospel the assembled chief priests and elders and scribes accuse

Jesus of precisely this sin: blasphemy! Mark 14:63-64). Jesus' word-become-deed of forgiveness of sin crossed a boundary! "The most important boundary the law provided was the one between God and creation ... Blasphemy is thus the most serious of all sins ... if Jesus is guilty of blasphemy, he must die."[2] Jesus had violated this boundary. He had blasphemed! This accusation hurled against Jesus (2:7) is a foreshadowing of what is to come. A shadow of death is cast over Jesus' journey from this moment on.

One other item of structural interest at this point is the possible relationship of these stories to the Parable of the Sower. We discussed Tolbert's hypothesis in the introduction, that the story of the Parable of the Sower is a kind of *plot synopsis* of chapters 1-10 of Mark's Gospel. Jesus' parable sets forth four kinds of "hearers of the word." Her contention is that the Pharisees fit the image of the first kind of hearer in Jesus' parable. The sower's first seeds were sown along the path where the birds came quickly and devoured them (Mark 4:4). In his explanation of this parable Jesus says that "these are the ones on the path where the word is sown: when they hear, Satan immediately comes and takes away the word that is sown in them" (Mark 4:15). Such a description certainly does seem to fit the Jewish religious leaders throughout these controversy stories in chapter 2. They see and hear this Jesus and (or so it would seem) Satan immediately puts it in their heads to raise a controversy.

Another theme in this story which links it to other Markan stories is the theme of authority. The very first response to Jesus' teaching was amazement at his authority, an authority not like that of the scribes (Mark 1:21-22). After he cast an unclean spirit out of a man the matter of his authority is raised again (Mark 1:27). In today's story the question of his authority is also raised. Jesus answers this issue with a statement which tells it true: " 'But so that you may know that the Son of Man has authority on earth to forgive sins' — he said to the paralytic — 'I say to you, stand up, take your mat and go to your home.' And he stood up ..." (Mark 2:10-12). This outspoken authority of Jesus will emerge again most especially when he enters Jerusalem (Mark 11:1ff.). He enters the temple and cleanses it and teaches with authority as Pharisees and

Sadducees pepper him with questions. The religious establishment didn't believe him in the beginning of the story. They didn't believe him in the end either. Speaking with authority, his fate is sealed.

Homiletical Directions

With this passage of Scripture those who wish to "think in story" are confronted with an incredible array of possibilities. Any of the themes we have traced above are ripe for story telling! We can tell stories which place this story as the climax of the healing stories. We can tell stories which see it as the beginning of the four controversy stories. We could follow Tolbert and bring in the Parable of the Sower here to understand what kind of hearers these Jewish religious leaders were. We could deal with the theme of blasphemy or authority. Good luck with any of them!

We have said little in this chapter about the two authoritative words of Jesus in this text: "Son, your sins are forgiven" (Mark 2:5); "I say to you, stand up, take up your mat and go to your home" (Mark 2:11). Either or both of these words calls us as preachers to speak for Jesus. Our listeners need to hear these words addressed to them personally in the midst of their need.

It might be best, therefore, to consider telling just one biblical story this week. Tell the story of this text in all of its richness. Take some time with it. Elaborate where necessary. A lot of explanatory comments can be *woven into the fabric of the story.* Explanation doesn't always call for us to stop the flow of the story for a mini-lecture on some finer point. The scribes accuse Jesus of blasphemy, for example. The explanation of blasphemy can be told as the thoughts of the scribes. "The scribes accused him of blasphemy," we might say, "thinking in their heads that blasphemy is that activity which crosses the line between Creator and creation." We could go on speculating on their thoughts. The point is simply that we can get said what blasphemy is all about without interrupting the flow of the story or leaving the story behind for a few minutes. This is an important task to master in the storytelling art.

Forgiveness of sins strikes very close to the heart and soul of the Christian proclamation. This is the only passage in Mark (and one of the few passages in the Gospels) where Jesus *announces* forgiveness of sins. The goal of our story on this pericope can well be that of shaping the telling of the story in such a way that this passage gets center stage. We can tell the story in such a way that this announcement of Jesus is heard several times. In the end of the matter what counts is that our congregations hear this word of Jesus addressed to them. This word of forgiveness does not need to be explained. It does not need to be followed up with all kinds of advice about what this forgiveness means in our life. At a fundamental level people simply need to hear this word of Jesus addressed to them over and over again.

A story is told about a couple celebrating their fiftieth wedding anniversary. In her comments the woman complained a bit that her husband simply had not told her he loved her very much. His reply: "I told you I loved you the day we were married. If anything changes, I'll let you know!" We all know that such an approach doesn't work. In a relationship of love we all need to hear the words of the beloved that say: "I love you." We never tire of hearing such a word! So it is with the simple word of Jesus which establishes, nourishes and sustains our relationship with him. "Your sins are forgiven," Jesus says. "I love you." We never tire of hearing that word. The old hymn has it right. As preachers we should love to tell the story of Jesus and his love. It's the only unique message we have to offer this world.

---

1. Mary Ann Tolbert, *Sowing the Gospel* (Minneapolis: Fortress Press, 1989), p. 140.

2. Donald H. Juel, *Mark* (Minneapolis: Augsburg Press, 1990), p. 47.

Mark 2:13-22

We may need to refresh our memory by noting that today's gospel text is one of four controversy stories in Mark 2:1—3:6. Jesus performed a burst of healings and exorcisms in chapter 1 which captured the admiration of the crowds (Mark 1:45; 2:12). With a new set of stories that end in 3:6 we find Jesus mired in constant controversy. These stories end on an ominous note (Mark 3:6). The leaders of the Jewish people come off in these stories in such a way as to suggest to some that they are the hearers of whom Jesus spoke in the Parable of the Sower when he said: "... when they hear, Satan immediately comes and takes away the word that is sown in them" (Mark 4:15).

Mary Ann Tolbert had noted for us that the section of Mark's Gospel which covers 1:16—2:12 begins with the calling of disciples and ends in amazement. So the section that commences in 2:13 also begins with the calling of disciples, though this section ends in 3:6 in the first rumblings of a plot to destroy Jesus. In the stories at the beginning of these sections *Jesus takes the initiative* in the calling of the disciples. In all the stories that are sandwiched in between the disciple-calling passages, *human beings take the initiative* in moving toward Jesus. People in their need come to Jesus with a cry for help. And Jesus helped! He healed and exorcized and forgave.

In 2:15-17 we have a brief story regarding Jesus' table manners. Table fellowship was a sacred matter in most of the ancient world. Table fellowship was the most intimate form of public fellowship imaginable. And here is Jesus transgressing boundaries again! He eats with tax collectors and sinners. He accepts Levi, a tax collector, an outcast in Jewish society, into his inner circle! The Pharisees were the keepers of the laws which established proper boundaries for the community of the religious. Jesus is clearly not very interested in this kind of stable community. He breaks down the boundaries, says Juel, in order to "... bring back the lost, heal the sick, cleanse the sinful." The time is fulfilled. The reign of God is near. God is at work in Jesus' gathering the lost! Jesus' word in this setting is certainly the gospel message *in nuce*; "Those who are well have no need of a physician, but those who are sick; I have come to call not the righteous but sinners" (Mark 2:17).

Something new is at hand! In Jesus' mind this is a time of feasting and celebration. It is a time of table fellowship where the sinners and outcast are welcome. It is not a time for fasting! The Pharisees had fasts. John's disciples had fasts. Jesus did not fast. The Pharisees wanted to know why. Jesus told them: "The wedding guests cannot fast while the bridegroom is with them, can they? As long as they have the bridegroom with them, they cannot fast" (Mark 2:19).

Something new is happening! That's Jesus' word to the Pharisees. This is a time of discontinuity. The new is incompatible with the old. You can't put the new wine into old wineskins. What Jesus is about, that is, is unprecedented in Israel. It is startling and unique. Sinners are welcome to the table! Such a thing was unheard of! Let's get it right. What is new is not that God loves sinners. What is new is that God loves sinners without waiting for them to become righteous and deserving. "... God proves his love for us in that while we still were sinners Christ died for us" (Romans 5:8).

Homiletical Directions

We have before us another passage of great richness and depth. The gospel message is here in a startling way. Let's not miss it! A first homiletical possibility would be to focus on the different sets of relationship to Jesus that are present in Mark's first two chapters. Story One can focus on the calling of the disciples. Tell the story in 1:16-20 and 2:13-14. Tell these stories in such a way that the *initiative of Jesus* is the focus of the telling. Here, too, Jesus speaks and it is so. The power of his authoritative word is manifest in calling disciples. Jesus says, "Follow me," and people follow.

Story Two can be a quick review of the stories in 1:21—2:12 where *people come to Jesus* to be healed, cleansed, forgiven. Tell these stories so that the focus is on *their initiative* in coming to Jesus in the midst of their desperate need.

Our logical minds might find a dilemma here. Which is it to be? Do we come to Jesus or does he come to us? This is one of many theological paradoxes which is probably best left unresolved. Both are true! In our lifelong relationship with Jesus there are times when his call to discipleship is paramount. "Follow me" is the word we hear. At other times in that relationship our needs are paramount. "Come to me" are the words we hear in those times.

The sermon might conclude, therefore, with these words of Jesus being addressed to our hearers. Jesus calls us to discipleship still today, we might say. Follow me. Deny yourself, take up your cross and follow! "Those who want to save their life will lose it, and those who lose their life for my sake, and for the sake of the gospel, will save it" (see Mark 8:34-35).

Jesus has another word for us today as well. "Come to me," he says. Come with your feelings that the hidden powers of this world have invaded your life. Come and hear Jesus say: "Come out."

Come with the uncleanness that mars your life. Come and hear Jesus say: "Be clean."

Come with the weight of your sins. Come and hear Jesus say: "Your sins are forgiven."

A second sermon possibility could focus on the events at the *welcome table*. Story One would be an elongated retelling of Mark 2:15-17. Put some of the background material about the nature of table fellowship in Jesus' day into your story. Let the focus of the story be on the nature of the welcome. Who is welcome at Jesus' table? "Those who are well have no need of a physician ... I have come to call not the righteous but sinners."

Stories Two and Three could be tellings of the stories of Jesus' feeding of the multitudes in Mark 6:30-44 and 8:1-9. Focus the telling of these stories on the same question as above: Who is welcome at Jesus' table? The answer is that everyone is welcome. "Those who are well have no need of a physician ... I have come to call not the righteous but sinners."

Story Four in this approach to the text would be a telling of the story of Jesus' institution of the Lord's Supper in Mark 14:12-25.

Telling of these stories would be particularly appropriate, of course, on a Communion Sunday. Jesus' table is set in our churches yet today. Who is welcome at Jesus' table? "Those who are well have no need of a physician ... I have come to call not the righteous but sinners."

Mark 2:23—3:6

The series of controversy stories comes to an end with today's text. Two stories are put together for this Sunday. Both stories deal with the proper keeping of the sabbath. The matter of sabbath keeping was a powerful issue for the early church as it reached out to include Gentiles within its community. In the first story Jesus and his disciples were going through the grainfields on the Sabbath day plucking ears of grain for food. It would appear that the Pharisees interpreted this activity as *reaping* the grain, which was expressly forbidden on the sabbath. The Pharisees pose the "why?" question of controversy stories: "... why are they doing what is not lawful on the Sabbath?"

Jesus answers that *what he does is based on who he is.* He tells the Pharisees a story. (Jesus is a story thinker!) It is a story about the Lord's Anointed in the Hebrew Bible; it is a story about David. In telling this story Jesus clearly equates himself with David. The implication of the story is that Jesus is like David. Jesus, too, is the Lord's Anointed: the Messiah. It is because of who he is that he does what he does on the Sabbath day! It is little wonder that the Pharisees decided that they must destroy such a man as this! (3:6).

For some unknown reason Jesus' story of David is told of a priest named Abiathar when the biblical reference in 1 Samuel 21:1-6 is to a priest by the name of Ahimelech. Saul was Israel's first Anointed One (1 Samuel 10:1). But God soon repented over this choice of Saul and rejected Saul as king of God's people (1 Samuel 15:22-23, 34). David was the newly Anointed One (1 Samuel 16:1-13 *[13]*). Having two men anointed as king over the people is a recipe for disaster. Saul was bitterly jealous of David (1 Samuel 18:7-9, 12). In his rage Saul set out to destroy David. The story of David and the priest, Ahimelech, takes place in this context. David is on the run from the king. He is weary. He asks the priest for food. "Give me five loaves of bread, or whatever is here," David demands of Ahimelech. Ahimelech gives him the bread. Only it is not just any bread. The priest was out of common bread and had only holy bread, the bread of the Presence. So David ate the holy, Presence, bread.

That's the story Jesus called to Pharisaic remembrance. Jesus seems to say through this story: "If David can do it, I can do it. David can do it because he was the Lord's Anointed. I can do it because I am the Lord's Anointed." And then comes Jesus' crucial word about the sabbath: "The sabbath was made for humankind, and not humankind for the sabbath; so the Son of Man is lord even of the sabbath." In other words, *human need* takes precedent over *religious law*. David knew that, too. The one who could sing for us, "The Lord is my Shepherd," knew instinctively that Shepherd God saw *his need* to be more important than *laws* about bread.

Jesus moves on to a synagogue on the sabbath. He is now in the holy place on the holy day! The Pharisees are watching carefully lest Jesus do some unholy thing on the sabbath. Jesus proceeds to do such an unholy thing: he heals a man with a withered hand. That did it. "The Pharisees went out and immediately conspired with the Herodians against him, how to destroy him." This ominous note brings the controversy stories to an end. Very clearly, however, the controversy will continue in other forms. We noted earlier that this dark note in 3:6 is in contrast to the end of the four healing stories (2:12) where the people are amazed and give glory to God. These two passages, Mark 2:12 and 3:6, seem to be summaries of the two parts of this section of the Gospel of Mark: 1:16—3:6. Jesus' ministry begins with a rush of miraculous activity which is met with human amazement. The "rush" doesn't last long, however. The response to Jesus quickly turns to controversy and plots to kill!

This foreboding note in 3:6 also points forward to rejections to come. In Mark 6:1-6 we hear of the rejection of Jesus by his hometown folks. In Mark 8:14-21 we hear of the incredible lack of understanding evidenced by the disciples. Jesus is rejected! That's the flow of Mark's story. It continues when Jesus enters Jerusalem (11:15-19). The Parable of the Tenants (12:1-11) strikes this note of rejection with particular clarity. (In the Preface it was noted that Mary Ann Tolbert sees this story as the "plot synopsis" of Mark 11-16.) The owner of the vineyard finally sends his "beloved son" to collect what is his, and the wicked tenants kill the beloved son.

Jesus closes this Parable by quoting Psalm 118:22-23: "The stone that the builders rejected has become the cornerstone; this was the Lord's doing, and it is amazing in our eyes" (Mark 12:10-11). Death is not to be the end of the story! God is at the end of this story with a marvelous surprise. But rejection and suffering and death are the markers along the way. (See also 8:31; 9:30-31; 10:32-34.) Mark's telling of the story of Jesus is a telling under the sign of the cross.

Homiletical Direction

A first possibility for preaching on this text from Mark would be to see it in its broadest setting in this Gospel. Mark 1:16—3:6 is clearly a complete cycle of material. The first half of this material leads to amazement. The second half leads to death threats. We indicated above where this rejection is present throughout Mark's story. As preachers we could tell some of these stories which clearly portray this gospel as a story of Jesus' march to Golgotha. There is a great African-American spiritual titled "Jesus Walked This Lonesome Valley." The song is tailor-made for this trail of texts in Mark. We could perhaps alter the title slightly for our homiletical purposes and have Jesus say these words: "I have walked this lonesome valley." This theme can be a thread that ties these various stories together. Some of the verses of the song could even be sung throughout the sermon. Experiments of splicing sermon and song together by this author have received highly favorable response from listeners.

After telling many of the Markan "lonesome valley" stories we can tell tales of our contemporary lonesome valleys. The good news of Mark's Gospel is that Jesus is portrayed as the Son of God who has walked this valley *by himself* but also *for us* and *with us*. "I have walked this lonesome valley for you," Jesus says. "I walk with you in your lonesome valleys. And when that valley ends in the shadow of death, there I will walk with you again into the sunshine of Easter's bright new morning."

A second sermonic possibility would be to focus on Jesus' relationship to the sabbath. Story One could be the David story from 1 Samuel 21. Let the focus of the story be on David's understanding that *human need* is more important than *laws about bread.* David knows who his Shepherd is, and the Good Shepherd is One who prepares a table for him even in the midst of his enemies. The God who is revealed in this story is a God who says: "I am a God who comes to break down religious laws in order to meet you in your need."

Stories Two and Three would be the two stories appointed for today. The focus should be on a God who also reveals through his Son that *human need* is more important than *religious law.* Repeat the theme in telling these stories: "I am a God who comes to break down religious laws in order to meet you in your need."

Story Four might be two or three brief stories of contemporary people and their need. The goal of the sermon's conclusion should be to have our proclamatory word speak to people in their need. People in all kinds of want need to hear God say: "I am a God who comes to break down religious laws in order to meet you in your need."

Finally, a sermon on healing could be preached on today's text using the second story of the healing of the man with the withered hand. Each year we march through many healing stories from our Gospels. Now and then we ought to focus on God as our healer. Jesus asks the Pharisees if it is lawful to *save life.* It is from these root words that we get our word *salvation.* In the New Testament salvation always includes the whole person. Salvation is not just for souls. Salvation is for bodies as well. Jesus has come to make bodies whole. Jesus has come as our healer.

We might see this as an instructional sermon about healing. Several points are always crucial when we discuss divine healing:

1. It is God's will to heal our bodies/selves and make us whole. The Bible is full of healing stories.

2. God's healing will finally come to all people in the resurrection on the last day. God will heal us!

3. We can pray in faith and in God's will that healing would come to us even now.

4. God's healing sometimes breaks out of the future and impinges on the present. People are healed in and through the faithful prayers of the Christian community.

5. The healing that comes does not depend on the authenticity of our faith. Healing comes because God chooses to set loose the power of resurrected life into our present age of dis-ease.

The worst sermon in the world, however, would be a sermon which makes all the right points about healing and utters no prayers for people to be healed. More and more churches are including prayers for healing in their hymnals. Invite people to come forward to be prayed for with the laying on of hands or the anointing with oil. In a congregation one Sunday the pastor explained that one of the committees of the church had asked him to have such healing prayers during a Sunday service. The pastor explained and explained what this would mean, clearly expecting that people were somewhat afraid and apprehensive about coming for such prayer. The pastor hoped his explanation would help. Whether due to his explanation or not, *everyone in the church that morning came forward*. People long to have prayers for healing.

An option to special prayers for healing would be to indicate clearly to the congregation that the Lord's Supper is a healing place. When we eat and drink the body and blood of Christ, when Christ enters our bodies, we can do so in expectant hope that our bodies might be healed! Every time we come to this table we can come with the expectation of healing.

Mark 3:20-35

Most commentators note that there is a break in the flow of Mark's story following our last pericope, which ended at Mark 3:6. The lectionary omits what follows immediately after 3:6, namely Mark 3:7-19. Mark 3:7-12 is, on the one hand, a kind of summary that pulls the threads of the story together. Such summaries are common in literature so closely based on orality.

On the other hand, verses 7-12 do move the story forward. References to the land "beyond" the Jordan and to Tyre and Sidon indicate that Jesus has taken his ministry into Gentile country. What happens in Gentile country is much like what happened in Jesus' first deeds of ministry among the Jews in Galilee. People *heard* the preaching of Jesus and they responded! In 1:21-28 a man with an unclean spirit was healed. This man recognized Jesus' identity. "I know who you are," the man said, "the Holy One of God" (Mark 1:24). Jesus commanded the man to be silent about this matter. Likewise, in Mark 3:7-12 the unclean spirits recognize Jesus as the Son of God. These spirits, too, are told not to make him known. In other words, this first foray of Jesus into Gentile country is a kind of parallel version of his first deeds of ministry in Jewish country.

We have spoken earlier of the "Son of God" motif in the Gospel of Mark. This passage is another instance of the revelation of Jesus' true identity, which is first known by demons and finally by the Roman Centurion (Mark 15:39).

In Mark 3:13-19 the theme of *insiders and outsiders* first emerges with the appointment of the twelve. This insider/outsider theme is found in many places in Mark's Gospel. From this point on in Mark's Gospel the story is as much about the insiders, about the twelve, as it is about Jesus. These twelve would appear to bear a special ministry to the people of the *twelve tribes:* Israel. We might also note that the appointment of the twelve took place on the "mountain." The mountain is often the place of the revelation of that which is new in scripture.

The ministry of the twelve is to be the ministry of the coming of the kingdom: preaching and casting out demons. The kingdom comes in word and deed! Needless to say, the twelve are appointed here to carry on the ministry that Jesus has already begun.

It is noted for us that Jesus gave Simon a new surname. Jesus called him Peter (Mark 3:16). Matthew uses this surname in a most positive way. Peter is the *rock on which the church is built.* (See Matthew 16:18.) Mary Ann Tolbert is convinced, however, that Mark uses this surname, Peter/rock, in a quite different way. In the Parable of the Sower one of the four kinds of soil is the *rocky* soil. Tolbert believes that in the telling of Mark's story it is the disciples who best fit this parable's description of *rocky ground.* [1]

One further note about these verses which are omitted from the lectionary but which contain important clues for Mark's story. The listing of the disciples concludes with the name of Judas Iscariot with the comment, "... who betrayed him" (Mark 3:19). Here is another of the ominous notes that Mark sprinkles throughout his Gospel. This is a story on the way to the cross!

The overall theme of the text appointed for Pentecost 4 is that of *rejection.* Jesus' friends think he is insane (3:21). The scribes who came down from Jerusalem think he must be possessed by a demon (3:22). His mother and brothers fail to grasp the meaning of his mission (3:31-35). The twelve are *insiders.* Jesus' friends and the scribes from Jerusalem and his mother and brothers appear to be *outsiders.* The message is not getting through.

What this means is that we have basically come through two entire chapters of Mark where, after initial amazement and reception (1:16—2:12), Jesus and the kingdom that he brings are rejected and misunderstood. We had the controversy stories in chapter 2. In chapter 3 we have his friends, the scribes, and his family who appear to be *outsiders* to his message. Jesus announced that he would bring the kingdom (1:15). But few believe. Even those who are insiders now, the twelve, will prove to be rocky ground for his message. *All of this sets the context for the crucially important Parable of the Sower.* Jesus understands *himself* to be the Sower, and he asserts in parabolic form (4:3-9) and in allegorical form

(4:14-20) that the soil of human hearts is turned against him for a variety of reasons.

But turned-against hearts will not stop the coming of the kingdom! There are some who are the good soil. In them the seed will yield unheard-of results: thirtyfold, sixtyfold and a hundredfold (4:8, 20). The kingdom will not be kept a secret forever (4:21-22). The kingdom of God is like a mustard seed. You don't see much at planting time but wait until you see what the harvest brings! "...when it is sown it grows up and becomes the greatest of all shrubs, and puts forth large branches, so that the birds of the air can make nests in its shade" (Mark 4:32). We shall deal with the Parable of the Sower in greater depth in chapter 12.

Now back to the scribes from Jerusalem (3:22ff.). Jesus was bringing the kingdom (Mark 1:15). The demons knew it! (Mark 1:24; 3:11). The darkness recognized the light. Death recognized the power of life. But the scribes don't get it. They assert that Jesus himself must be possessed by a demon. "He has Beelzebul, and by the ruler of the demons he casts out demons" (3:22). Jesus answered their charge by telling stories! The conclusion of his stories is that the scribes have committed blasphemy. Jesus, himself, had been accused of blasphemy in his first encounter with the scribes (2:6-7). Here Jesus turns the tables upon his accusers. "... Whoever blasphemes against the Holy Spirit can never have forgiveness, but is guilty of an eternal sin ..." (3:29). The scribes had committed the sin against the Holy Spirit. They committed this sin by claiming that Jesus had an unclean spirit (3:22, 30).

The "sin against the Holy Spirit" has received much attention in the Christian community through the ages. It has been clear to Christian people that the sin against the Holy Spirit brings with it the most serious consequences of all. A common question among Christians is the question of the specific nature of this sin. Christian teachers have come up with all kinds of answers for the meaning of the "sin against the Holy Spirit." It is best to forget any answers we might have learned about this most grievous sin. In this text in Mark's Gospel the sin against the Holy Spirit is clearly defined. If we name Jesus wrongly, we commit the sin against the Spirit. If we say Jesus has an unclean spirit, when in fact he has the Holy

Spirit, we have sinned against the Spirit. All of this makes ultimate sense. Jesus is the one who comes bringing the kingdom, casting out demons, forgiving sinners. Since forgiveness comes in Jesus' name, no forgiveness can come to a person who takes this name in vain. Misnaming Jesus is an eternal sin. It is blasphemy. Blasphemy shuts us out of the kingdom-come-near in Jesus' name.

Homiletical Directions

Among many possible approaches to this week's text, one would deal with the matters at hand quite broadly; another might focus more narrowly on the "sin against the Holy Spirit." The broad approach could seek to tell the whole story of Mark from 1:14— 4:34. You will have worked with many of these passages in earlier sermons so there is no need to tell all these stories in their completeness. Brief allusions can suffice. The story begins with the coming of the kingdom and initial acceptance, indeed, amazement! (Mark 1:16-2:12). Then come the controversy stories with a first hint of a plot forming against Jesus (Mark 2:1—3:6). The stories in Mark 3 focus on *rejection* by friends, scribes and family. This presents us with the context for the Parable of the Sower. In this parable Jesus indicates that much of the ground upon which his seed is sown is poor soil for his message. Jesus goes on, however, to tell us that the seed of the gospel of the kingdom will produce thirtyfold, sixtyfold and a hundredfold in some hearers. The kingdom of God is like a mustard seed! It might look small and insignificant now, but just wait and see the harvest that will come!

This larger bracket of stories can be related to our hearers in several ways. We might have our stories focus on the difficulty with which the message of the coming kingdom is met by even those closest to Jesus. Is it any different in our day? Jesus' message is rejected by many in our time. Each hearer of the word can be challenged to place him/herself in relation to these stories. What kind of hearer am I? The kingdom will triumph, the seed will grow, but will I be included? Or, for those who understand themselves as the good soil, the good news is that rejection of Jesus is just for a time and then the secret will be revealed to all (Mark

4:21-23). The kingdom is coming. The kingdom will prevail. This is a message of patience and hope for the good-soil folk.

It is difficult, however, to pass up a narrower focus for today's sermon. We have this "sin against the Holy Spirit" reality before us. This kind of rejection of Jesus' message appears to be far more grievous than other forms of rejection we have seen in the early chapters in Mark. For this rejection there is no forgiveness. This sin is eternal!

The story in 3:20-30 might be the story for the sermon today. Tell just this story. Tell it in its fullness. Set it in its context in Mark. Let explanations of words like Beelzebul and blasphemy be woven into the strand of the story. Tell it in such a way that it emerges clearly from the telling that Jesus' definition of the "sin against the Holy Spirit" is the sin of misnaming him. When we fail to recognize the spirit that truly animates this Son of God we place ourselves beyond his forgiving reach; we become guilty of an eternal sin.

After telling this story it might be a good idea to track some of the ways the church has taught on the subject of the "sin against the Holy Spirit." It would be even more important to name the anxiety that lies deep in many a troubled breast that this sin, whatever it is, might keep them from God's offer of forgiveness. It would be of crucial importance that a sermon on this theme conclude with a word of forgiveness spoken by you to the congregation *in Jesus' name.*

We might say something like this in the conclusion of our sermon: "Jesus is not possessed by Beelzebul as the scribes maintained. Jesus is not possessed by an unclean spirit. Jesus is filled with the Holy Spirit. It is through the present power of the Holy Spirit that Jesus' words of old have power yet today. Jesus' word to us is the same yesterday, today, forever. 'I forgive you all your sin,' he says to each and every one of us today. If you can believe these words, you have it. Forgiveness of sins is yours, now, as a free gift. Such faith in the word of Jesus precisely marks you as a person who has not committed the sin against the Holy Spirit. You cannot believe in Jesus' word of forgiveness and commit the sin against the Holy Spirit at the same time! That's impossible. So hear his word once more. It is spoken just for you. It offers you life now and for all eternity. The word is simply: 'I forgive you all your sins.' Amen."

---

1. Mary Ann Tolbert, *Sowing the Gospel* (Minneapolis: Fortress Press, 1989), p. 45.

Chapter 12
The Parable Of The Sower

Mark 4:1-20

We have indicated a number of times that the Parable of the Sower plays a crucial role in the overall structure of Mark's Gospel. One aspect of its importance is the amount of space it takes up in Mark's Gospel. It can be argued that Mark 4:1-34 is part of a whole in this crucial teaching of Jesus. Another aspect of the parable's importance is that it is told *twice*. Jesus tells the parable (4:3-9). Then he explains the parable (Mark 4:14-20). The second telling is more of an allegory.

In the Preface we set forth some basic realities about this parable based on the insights of Donald Juel and Mary Ann Tolbert. Tolbert comes to her study of Mark with a background of research in the ancient novels of the Hellenistic world of Jesus' day. She believes that it is possible to assume that the readers of Mark's Gospel were familiar with this genre of literature. She is convinced, furthermore, that the Gospel of Mark has many similarities to these ancient novels. She concludes her remarks in this area with the following summary:

> *While the Gospel of Mark and the early examples of the ancient novel obviously do not share the same story line, their rhetorical, stylistic, and linguistic similarities are conspicuous. Both are synthetic, conventional narratives that combine historiographic form with epic and dramatic substance. Episodic plots, central turning points, final recognition sequences, dialogic scenes with narrative frames, sparing but crucial use of monologue, repetition, narrative summaries, foreshadowing, and monolithic, illustrative characters are some of the elements the Gospel and ancient novels have in common ... If the Gospel of Mark is an example of Hellenistic popular literature, we have uncovered a major reason for its opacity and*

apparent muddle for modern readers ... If Mark is a popular literary text, modern readers absolutely must discern some of the competencies of the authorial audience in order to have any hope of following the story. [1]

We cannot, in a work of this nature, pursue each line of endeavor that Tolbert outlines. One of the characteristics of ancient novels and the Gospel of Mark is the use of *plot synopses*. We touched upon this in the Preface. Tolbert sees these plot synopses as a key to unlock the overall meaning of Mark's narrative. She identifies the two lengthy parables told in Mark's Gospel as the keys to the plot of the entire narrative. These parables are the Parable of the Sower and the Parable of the Wicked Tenants (12:1-12). She asserts that the Parable of the Sower is the plot synopsis of the first ten chapters of Mark; the Parable of the Tenants is the plot synopsis of the last six chapters. This analysis fits the "geography" of Mark's narrative. The first ten chapters take place in Galilee. The last six chapters occur in Jerusalem. So it may be that each "geographical" area of the Gospel contains a parable or parables of Jesus which summarize the plot thereof.

Jesus' story of the Sower is the first time in the Gospel that we have before us a sustained teaching of Jesus. This alone marks it as important! We set the context for the parable in the last chapter in discussing the two chapters (Mark 2 and 3) of constant rejection of Jesus and his mission. It is helpful to see the Parable of the Sower in this context. Rejection of the coming reign of God is answered by agricultural stories of the coming reign of God. Much of the soil on which the Sower sows the seed is not good soil. That's the problem. But, in spite of this problem, there will be in many hearts an exceedingly abundant harvest: thirtyfold, sixtyfold, a hundredfold! The coming of God's reign is not a lamp to hide under a bushel! God's reign is a light that should show forth throughout the whole world (Mark 4:21-22). "Let anyone with ears to hear listen!" (Mark 4:23).

This plea to listen is a key part of the story of the Sower and of Mark's Gospel. The parable begins with an imperative: Listen! It ends with an imperative: "Let anyone with ears to hear listen!"

(Mark 4:9). In Jesus' interpretation of the parable it is clear that the parable is told about different kinds of *hearing*. The Sower sows the word. Some hear and some don't hear. It may look for a time that no one is listening. But the harvest will come in incredible plenty.

The verses between the telling of the parable and its allegorical explanation are difficult (Mark 4:10-13). Those who listen to Jesus are the *insiders*. To them the secret of the kingdom has been given. For the *outsiders* everything is in parables "... in order that 'they may indeed look, but not perceive, and may indeed listen, but not understand; so that they may not turn again and be forgiven'" (Mark 4:12). These are hard words from the Old Testament story of the call of the prophet Isaiah (Isaiah 6:9-10). There is no escaping the intent of these words. Jesus intends that a veil be cast over the minds of many at the sound of his word. Juel puts the matter thus:

> *God alone can open eyes and ears, and will not. The present, Isaiah is told, is a time of veiling and punishment. There seems no escape from the implication: God has the sovereign right to determine who will and who will not see and hear — and repent ... [Jesus] intends — at least at this stage in his ministry — to keep outsiders in the dark ... The one who told parables was hung on a cross. That does not remove the offense, however, it only deepens the mystery ... The statement is of a piece with Jesus' silencing of the demons and his injunctions to people he has healed not to make him known. We are not given an explanation of his reasons ... We learn only a few verses later that Jesus' ultimate intention is not veiling and concealment. The goal of his mission is disclosure. Nothing is hid except to be made manifest (4:22). The story is headed somewhere. Jesus' sowing will lead ultimately to the harvest ... .[2]*

Juel also helps us interpret the soil. There are many readings of this parable which put much emphasis on the soil. We must be good soil! We must be good listeners! We must get it right! Juel sees a problem here. *A promise has been turned into a demand.* Soil, he maintains, is a *passive* image. "The soil will produce —

not because it can make some Herculean effort but because it is good soil and the farmer knows his business."[3] This promise of a harvest stands over the rest of Mark's story. What we do not know at this juncture of the story is for whom the promise is intended. Who are the ones who listen and believe? Who are the good soil people? We don't know. We have heard and are called to believe that the promise will bear fruit. There is more to this story! We must read on.

In another work, Juel turns his mind to this parable. He reminds us again of how crucial the narrative setting is for understanding the parable. We must remember two things about this parable above all else. "First, the parable needs to be read as speaking about the Kingdom of God. It is, after all, God's work that the parable — and the Gospel — seek to understand ...Second, the parable is interpreted as having to do with reception of the Word."[4] The emphasis here is on *reception.* The emphasis in the parable is on what kinds of hearers we are. Hearing is *passive*! It does not depend upon human efforts! The kingdom comes through the work of the Sower and not through the work of the soil!

This is true of the Gospel writer, Mark, as well. His Gospel sows the seed. It doesn't end. There is no ending to this Gospel. Just sowing. Sowing that ultimately falls upon our hearts. At this point we must simply trust the promise of the parable that the harvest will be plentiful in our lives and in the lives of all who hear. Faith comes through what is heard!

In the Preface reference was made to Tolbert's attempts to align the characters in other stories in the Gospel as examples of different kinds of hearing.[5] In examining the Gospel she finds that the scribes, the Pharisees, the Herodians, and the Jerusalem Jews are examples of seed sown on the way, seed sown that Satan immediately takes away. Tolbert has said that once we have the plot synopsis of the Parable of the Sower we ought to be on the lookout for people in Mark's story who are like these different kinds of soil. For the ancient reader/listener the suspense in a story was not about what would happen. They knew that from the plot synopsis. What they didn't know was how the plot would play itself out. We can be alert, as well, to stories that relate to the different kinds of soil. An occasional sermon in the year of Mark might work with these narrative connections.

For the seed sown in *rocky* ground Tolbert turns to the disciples as exemplars. We have noted earlier her identification of Simon, surnamed Peter/*rock* by Jesus, with the rocky ground that is the disciples. Rocky ground people respond *immediately* to the sowing of the word. When the first disciples were called it was noted that *immediately* they followed Jesus (Mark 1:18). Another link to the disciples is the language in the parable of *falling away* (Mark 4:17). This is just the language Jesus uses of the disciples in Mark 14:27, 29. On this basis Tolbert identifies the disciples, especially Peter, James and John, as the exemplars of the rocky ground.

The exemplars of those sown among the thorns are the rich man in Mark 10:17-22 and King Herod, Mark 6:14-29. [The story of Pilate might well be added to this list (Mark 15:1-15).] Both the rich man and Herod are sorry for what they are asked to do. Both men are prevented from acting on their better instincts by other things. "... The cares of the world, and the lure of wealth, and the desire for other things come in and choke the word, and it yields nothing" (Mark 4:19). A sermon on these two men (and also Pilate?) in relation to the thorny ground might be very relevant in our day. The cares of the world, the lust for wealth and the desire for other things live strong in our land! (See chapter 17).

And the good soil. Tolbert's identification of these hearers focuses primarily on the three stories in Mark 5. Before we come to these stories, however, we must note the story told in Mark 4:35-41. In this story the disciples stand before the two possibilities of life in the presence of the coming-near reign of God. They can evidence *fear* or they can have *faith*. The disciples will be seen to be people of fear quite often in Mark's story. But the people in Mark 5 — a man who lives in the Greek cities of the Decapolis and is possessed by a demon, a poor woman with a flow of blood, and a leader of a Jewish synagogue — are people of *faith*. In them the word produces thirtyfold, sixtyfold and a hundredfold.

It is quite amazing to look again at the narrative context of the Parable of the Sower. The chapters leading up to this parable tell story after story of the rejection of Jesus. The Parable of the Sower is addressed to this rejection and indicates that some soil is not ripe for the reception of the kingdom, but the day will come when an abundant harvest bursts forth. Mark 5 seems to chronicle the abundant harvest! All of a sudden, following the parable, people respond to Jesus and amazing fruit is borne in their bodies. There is much fruit for narrative preaching of gospel stories here!

At the end of her analysis of the four kinds of soil, Tolbert makes an interesting assertion about the kingdom of God in Mark. She is convinced that the Greek word for kingdom (*basileia*) stands behind Mark's thinking. The Greek word for kingdom, in contrast with the Aramaic word, has a stronger *spatial perspective.*

> *By explicating the kingdom of God through the metaphor of good earth, Mark appears to be developing the concept in its Greek form ... For Mark, the kingdom of God is God's ground which produces of itself and in transforming abundance. It is not so much God's reign that is at issue but the land over which God legitimately rules, a land that has at least in part been usurped by evil powers ... The parables of the Four Types of Earth ... demonstrate a remarkable confluence of ground imagery for the kingdom of God: it is the good earth that yields fruit; the earth that, once sown, produces of itself; the earth that can transform a tiny seed into a magnificent bush; and a lovingly created and planted vineyard now in the hands of tenants who refuse to provide fruit to the lord of the vineyard.* [6]

Still, Tolbert notes, the agricultural metaphor for the kingdom can be taken too far. "... The mystery of the kingdom is not agricultural but human. It is the human heart, not land, that is the seat of God's domain." [7]

Mark tells the story of the Sower of the Word who liberally sows his seed on human hearts. If anything, the story is left in mystery concerning human response to the generosity of the Sower. Always, always, Mark's story ends in human hearts, in our human heart. The promise of the Sower is that this sowing will one day produce an abundant harvest in our lives. We are among those privileged to be called to sow this Word on the soil of human hearts. We sow the word trusting in the promise of the Sower!

---

1. Mary Ann Tolbert, *Sowing The Gospel* (Minneapolis: Fortress Press, 1989), pp. 78-79.

2. Donald H. Juel, *Mark* (Minneapolis: Augsburg Press, 1990), pp. 71-72.

3. *Ibid.*, p. 75.

4. Donald H. Juel, *A Master of Surprise* (Minneapolis: Fortress Press, 1994), p. 59.

5. Mary Ann Tolbert, *Sowing the Gospel* (Minneapolis: Fortress Press, 1989), pp. 148-175. Material in this section is dependent on Tolbert's discussion.

6. *Ibid.*, p. 172.

7. *Ibid.*, p. 173.

Mark 4:26-34

We come now to the Sunday of the "great omission." Lectionary Cycle B skips over the first 25 verses of Mark 4: the Parable of the Sower. In chapter 12 we have given consideration to this parable at some length. Many interpreters see this parable as one of the keys for interpreting Mark's Gospel in its overall, narrative sense. We must find room in our preaching on Mark's Gospel to include the Parable of the Sower. This might be the Sunday for such inclusion.

It is not only the Parable of the Sower that has been omitted. Mark 4:21-25 has also been omitted. We commented on the theme of these verses in chapter 12. In his words to the disciples Jesus had said some things about who will hear and believe that are difficult to grasp. The Twelve, the insiders, can know the secrets of the kingdom. Those who are outside cannot figure it out. They see but they do not perceive. They hear but they don't understand (Mark 4:10-12). Mark 4:21-25 helps to interpret these hard-to-grasp verses. This story "talks" to that story. "... There is nothing hidden, except to be disclosed; nor is anything secret, except to come to light. Let anyone with ears to hear listen!" (Mark 4:22-23). When these stories are allowed to have conversation with each other we begin to catch Jesus' full message.

The matter of hearing is also emphasized again in 4:21-25. The Parable of the Sower had begun and ended with a call to listen. That is true because what the Sower sows is the *word*. A word is offered to be heard. Faith comes through such hearing. This relationship between hearing and faith will be evident throughout Mark's Gospel.

The parables before us this week are clearly related to each other and to the Parable of the Sower. Mark 4 is a long meditation on matters of sowing and harvest. When we attach these parables to the Parable of the Sower we hear that the sowing of the Sower (Jesus) is most certainly not in vain. Some seed falls on the path, some on rocky ground and some amongst the thorns, to be sure. But other seed produces extravagantly: thirtyfold, sixtyfold, a hundredfold. The seed sprouts and grows even though the farmer doesn't understand the process at work here. In some instances the seed is very small. "Not to worry," says Jesus, "for from very small seeds come the greatest shrubs of all."

We could put these stories under our usual exegetical microscope and come up with all kinds of interesting information. Such a course of investigation may well produce more harm than good. These parables in today's text are not given primarily for our analysis. They are given as words of proclamation and hope. That is how we shall treat them.

Homiletical Directions

Let's make this Sunday the time to begin to unfold the riches of the Parable of the Sower. You may wish to refer to the previous chapter to call some of these riches to mind. Of most concern is the overall context of the Markan story through Mark 4:34. Mark chapters 2 and 3 are filled with stories of the rejection of Jesus. That can be Story One for this week's sermon. We don't need to tell all the stories in these chapters. Tell enough and summarize others so that hearers get the message that coming to the Parable of the Sower we are faced with massive rejection of the One who announced that in his ministry the reign of God had drawn near.

Story Two is a place we might tell the Parable of the Sower. It would appear that one of the reasons Jesus has for telling this parable is as a logical answer to the questions raised in chapters 2-3. What's going on here? Wasn't Jesus supposed to be Son of God, bringer of the kingdom? Why all the rejection? What does it all mean? And the answer is: the Parable of the Sower! If you can set up the context for this parable in telling the rejection stories in chapters 2-3 you need make little further comment on the Sower's story. It speaks for itself.

If you wish to nudge it along to clarity, focus on the fact that it is true (at least for a time) that some people just don't get it. Some people are path people; Satan snatches the word they have heard from them. Others are rocky ground people; they follow immediately but they have no depth and they fall away when times of trial come upon them. Still others are thorny ground people; they hear the word with joy, but the cares of the world and the delight in riches choke out the word. But! There are also the good soil people; they bear fruit in manifold abundance. All is not lost! What is secret will come to light.

Story Three can be the telling of today's parables in context. It is recommended that you simply proclaim these parables. Don't read them, though. Have them memorized or tell them in your own words. You've told Story One (rejection) and Story Two (some reject but some bear fruit). These stories of rejection and wondering about the coming of the reign of God are not just yesterday's stories! We ask the same questions today. Faith is constantly confronted with the fulfillment gap between the promises of Jesus and the reality of our faith-lives. Mark knew this very well. He presents Jesus, therefore, as the One who must suffer. (See Mark 8:31; 9:30-31; 10:32-34 and the Passion story!) Mark's Jesus is the Crucified. Mark's Jesus is the One who reveals himself in dying on a cross. Mark knew that the Sower himself would one day be sown in the earth. And yet there is hope! Seed that is sown will spring forth and blossom even a hundredfold!

A host of contemporary questions come to mind:
In the light of Jesus' bringing the kingdom near …
Why is there still war and rumors of war?
Why do humans continue to do great harm to the environment?
Why is hate lodged so deep in human hearts?
Why do human relationships constantly fall apart?
Why do I suffer?
Add your own items to this list.

We are tempted to *reject* Jesus in light of these and many other realities. In your sermon lift up at least four of these kinds of questions for your hearers. You can lift them up in brief story form or by simply citing them. After putting forth the first question on your list, simply tell the story in vv. 26-29. Tell it as proclamation. Tell it as the answer to the question. Be sure in your telling that you emphasize that this is what *the kingdom of God is like.* (Remember: don't read it.)

Raise your second question. After you have enunciated it, tell the story from vv. 30-32. Again, tell it as proclamation.

Raise your third question. Tell the parable in vv. 26-29 again. Trust the power of oral repetition!

Raise your fourth question. Tell the parable in vv. 30-32 again. Say, "Amen." Let Jesus' parables speak for themselves.

Mark 4:35-41

In the overall structure of Mark's Gospel we now move into material that follows the Parable of the Sower, which is the plot synopsis of the first ten chapters of Mark. This story of the disciples in the boat, along with the whole of Mark 5, is about different kinds of soil. The Sower sows the word and people hear and receive that word in different ways. The rocky-ground disciples are *afraid.* Fear is one of the fundamental responses to the Sower in Mark's story. Mark's Gospel, in fact, ends with a note of fear! (Mark 16:8: "… and they [the women] said nothing to anyone, for they were *afraid.*") In this story the disciples and Jesus get into a boat for a trip to the other side of the lake. Wind and sea rose up in fury. The disciples were afraid they would perish in this storm. Jesus, on the other hand, was not afraid. He was asleep! One wonders if this is a kind of flash-forward to Gethsemane, when it was the disciples who could not keep watch. They fell asleep three times (Mark 14:32-42).

After the disciples awoke Jesus, he spoke a personal word to his friends, the wind and sea, and the storm subsided. There are Old Testament parallels to this power of God over the forces of nature. See for example Job 38:1-11; Psalm 74:13-14; 107:23-29. The Creator has the final word over the creation! In relationship to the forces of nature Jesus acts as God acts. Truly this man is the Son of God!

We will focus our remarks on this text upon the disciples and their response to Jesus. "Why are you afraid?" Jesus asked them. "Have you still no faith?" This contrast between faith and fear as alternative responses to the work and word of the Sower is woven throughout Mark's Gospel. In the stories of Mark 5, for example, we hear this refrain over and over again. The townspeople were *afraid* (5:15) in light of Jesus' healing of the Gerasene demoniac.

When Jesus goes to the home of Jairus to heal his daughter he tells the people gathered round: "Do not *fear*, only believe" (5:36). Jesus commends the woman with the flow of blood who was healed as she desperately reached out and touched the hem of his garment. Jesus said to her: "Daughter, your *faith* has made you well ..." (5:34). The stories told in Mark 5 are clearly stories of people who are "good soil" in whom the harvest is thirtyfold, sixtyfold and hundredfold. They are people of faith, not of fear.

We will come upon other instances of this faith/fear polarity in the course of Mark's Gospel. Mark seems to pose these realities as the basic alternatives of hearing in response to the work/word of the Sower. The kingdom of God draws near when the word falls on good (receptive) soil. Mary Ann Tolbert says that,

> *Mark 4:1-34 supplies the audience with the fundamental typology of hearing-response that organizes the entire plot of the Gospel ... While Mark 4:1-34 reflects this theological vision in the symbolic or parabolic categories of nature, such as sown seed and productive or unproductive earth, the purpose of the Gospel narrative as a whole is to portray it in human form.* [1]

This story of the disciples and Jesus in the boat is the first of three boat stories in Mark's Gospel. Each boat story paints the disciples in terms of their fear and unbelief. These stories appear in Mark 6:45-52 and 8:14-21. Neither story is a part of this year's lectionary cycle. In the homiletical section below, therefore, we will propose the telling of the three disciple/boat stories as the structure of this week's sermon.

These boat stories do not flatter the disciples. If anything, they buttress the suggestion that the disciples are the rocky-ground hearers. They fear. They do not believe. Their hearts are hardened. In the story in Mark 6 the disciples are on the sea, distressed in their rowing. So Jesus walks out to them! The disciples see him and are filled with *fear*. Jesus seeks to comfort them in their fear. He says to them: "Take heart, it is I; do not be *afraid*" (6:50). Surely by now the disciples will catch on. Maybe the next verse will tell us that they finally put their fears behind them and came to faith. No such luck! "And they were utterly astounded, for they did not understand about the loaves, but their hearts were hardened" (6:51-52). They still don't get it. Their hearts are impervious. Their hearts are hardened; they are the rocky soil!

The third boat scene (Mark 8:14-21) is even more astonishing. It is a story set up by Jesus' second feeding of the multitudes. After the second such feeding of the crowd, the disciples get into the boat with Jesus again. We prepare for the worst! The worst is what we get. Incredibly, the disciples seem worried over the fact that they have only one loaf of bread. It was only in hearing Mark's Gospel story told orally from start to finish that the irony of this story jumped out at this author. Studying these stories in isolation from each other often prevents us from seeing the big picture. The big picture here is that Jesus fed the multitudes twice. (See chapter 6:30-44 and 8:1-10.) Each time there are a lot of leftovers. Twelve baskets of leftovers in chapter 6, seven baskets of leftovers in chapter 8. And then we hear the disciples being afraid for their hunger because they only have one loaf! When the stories of the feedings and the disciples' fear that they have only one loaf are told together, they strike us with comic effect!

Jesus' words to the disciples in this boat story are mind-boggling. To his *disciples* he says, "Why are you talking about having no bread? Do you still not perceive or understand? Are your hearts hardened? (Rocky ground!) Do you have eyes, and fail to see? Do you have ears, and fail to hear?" (Mark 8:17-18). What is astonishing about this speech of Jesus is that it is the *reversal* of what he had said in explaining the Parable of the Sower to the disciples. There he had said that the disciples were the *insiders* who get to know the *secret,* the kingdom of God. The *outsiders*, on the other hand, would see, but not perceive. The *outsiders* would hear, but not understand (Mark 4:11-12). In this story, however, it is the insiders, the disciples themselves, who are as outsiders. They have eyes, but they do not see. They have ears, but they do not understand.

Homiletical Directions

The proposal for preaching this week is to tell the three boat stories that we have looked at above. These stories need to be told

94

in context with each other, and this is the only chance to do so because the boat stories in Mark 6 and 8 do not appear in Lectionary Cycle B.

Two suggestions for the telling of these stories: In the telling let the disciples appear as Mark paints them. These *insiders* appear as *outsiders*. Those who should have *faith* are filled with *fear*. The disciples are rocky ground; their hearts are hardened. After telling the three stories we can raise some questions with our congregation. What kind of hearers are we? Are we insiders who can become outsiders? Do we have faith or fear in our hearts? Are we rocky ground after all? These questions, of course, can be fleshed out in more detail.

Close the sermon with prayer. Pray for the Holy Spirit to touch the lives of all assembled. Pray for the Holy Spirit to work with the seed that has been sown on these human hearts. Pray for the Holy Spirit to turn our hearts from fear to faith. Pray for the Holy Spirit to open our eyes that we might truly see; to open our ears that we might truly understand. A hymn that sings of the assurance that the Sower, Jesus Christ, watches carefully over the seed that has been sown might be sung in conclusion.

A second approach would be like the first in that the three boat stories would be told. Instead of ending with a prayer, however, we would end with the final story in Mark's Gospel. Things look pretty grim for these "boat people," these disciples. And it gets worse. Three times they will respond to Jesus' revelation that he must suffer and be crucified with their own preference to live in present glory. Three times they respond to his call to "watch" by falling asleep. There is this interesting pattern of "threes" in Mark's Gospel as he paints the disciples in bleak tones.

The implication of the telling of these stories, of course, is that there are many among us today who might feel like the disciples. Our hearts are hard. Our soil is rocky. Our eyes don't always see the things of faith. Our ears don't always hear properly. We often live in fear, not trusting faith. Is there any hope for us?

YES! The disciples are not left to fade into disgrace with their threefold patterns of hardened hearts, denial and betrayal. At the end of the story the young man at the tomb speaks Jesus' good-news word for the disciples: "... go, tell his disciples and Peter that he is going ahead of you to Galilee; there you will see him, just as he told you" (Mark 16:7). The final word to hard-hearted, "rocky ground" disciples is a word of hope and promise. Jesus has spoken this word for hard-hearted disciples in every age.

We can put these words in Jesus' mouth as the climax of our sermon. Jesus' word is a word for fearful, hard-hearted disciples in our time. It is a word for those who hear us sow the word of these stories. Jesus says to all of us today:

"I am going before you to Galilee. I have more seeds to sow upon your 'rocky ground' hearts. I have more seeds to sow that your ears might hear and your eyes might see. I have more seeds to sow to turn your fear to faith. I refuse to leave you in your hard-hearted condition. Come on along to Galilee. I have more seeds to sow. Amen."

---

1. Mary Ann Tolbert, *Sowing The Gospel* (Minneapolis: Fortress Press, 1989), pp. 163-164.

Mark 5:21-43

The revised lectionary cycle serves us well by putting the intercalated stories of the healing of the unclean woman with the flow of blood and the raising of the twelve-year-old girl together again. We still have the problem, however, that vv. 1-20 are omitted totally from the lectionary readings. It can be argued on a number of premises that these three stories belong together. They belong together, for example, as a threefold response to the question of the disciples: "Who then is this, that even the wind and the sea obey him?" (Mark 4:41). Who is this? This is the One who brings the kingdom near by casting out a legion of demons, healing a woman with a twelve-year flow of blood and raising a twelve-year-old girl from the dead!

Mary Ann Tolbert suggests another reason for holding these three stories together. She sees them as examples of the *good soil* that Jesus alluded to in his Parable of the Sower. She includes the story of the disciples in Mark 4:35-41 in her grouping together of these stories. "These four episodes, by contrasting the disciples to three people seeking healing, distinguish the rocky ground from the good earth and the human response of fear from the healing one of faith."[1] We recall the response of the disciples to Jesus as one of *fear.* The stories in Mark 5 are stories of people who come to Jesus for healing. They are stories of people of *faith.* These may well be Mark's best examples of *good soil people*!

The location of the story in Mark 5:1-20 is "on the other side of the sea" in the country of the Gerasenes. This is Gentile country! The Gentiles, of course, are outsiders to the promises for Israel. The man with the demon is an *outsider even to these Gentile outsiders*!! He is a man with an unclean spirit who lived among the tombs. Jesus has come to bind the "strong one" in the land of the Gerasenes, just as he did in the first miracle he performed in

97

Capernaum (1:21-28). Jesus is the kingdom of God drawn near. As an agent of the coming kingdom Jesus sets his will against evil first in Capernaum among the people of Israel, then in the land of the Gerasenes among Gentiles.

In doing this deed on Gentile soil Jesus cleanses the land. He does this most massive of his exorcisms on Gentile land and follows it up with the greatest miracle he ever did for a person (raising the dead!) on Jewish land. Jesus, therefore, embraces both sides of the sea! The coming kingdom is a kingdom that includes all people! Jesus has broken the boundaries again. He has transgressed the barriers that had labeled Gentiles as outsiders.

Tolbert's thesis is that the Gerasene demoniac is the first example Mark gives us of a *good soil* person. She sees each of the stories in Mark 5 as stories told to illustrate who the "good soil" people are. The demoniac is the first "good soil" person. His malady is described in great detail. And what can he do about it? He can run to Jesus. He ran and fell down before Jesus out of his desperation. Jesus saw his faith and said, "Come out of the man, you unclean spirit!" The demoniac shouted at Jesus in response: "What have you to do with me, Jesus, Son of the Most High God? I adjure you by God, do not torment me" (Mark 5:7). After a brief conversation, Jesus cast out the legion of demons from the unclean man and sent them into the unclean pigs. A great Gentile cleansing had occurred! The townspeople, however, did not get it. They saw the man in his right mind and they were *afraid* (5:15). We have here again the contrast between *faith* and *fear*. Remember Jesus and the disciples (4:40).

Jesus let the faithful man tell his story (5:19). Others had been told *not to tell* (1:34, 44; 2:12). The cleansed Gentile demoniac is allowed to speak. Is this because Jesus is in Gentile land? In this land the word about Jesus needs to be heard. There is a kind of foreshadowing of the preaching to the Gentiles in this story.

The second story of a good soil person is Jairus, a ruler of the synagogue. Jesus had crossed the sea again (5:21) and is back in Jewish territory. This is the first time in Mark's story that a respectable person from the Jewish community has taken any interest in Jesus! You find good soil people in the strangest places!

Jairus' daughter is near death. Like the Gerasene demoniac, Jairus comes to Jesus in the midst of his desperate need. He comes in faith. He believes that Jesus can help. "Come and lay your hands on her, so that she may be made well, and live" (Mark 5:23). There is great urgency in this story. The girl is near death. But on the way to Jairus' house Jesus' entourage encounters a delay. A woman with a twelve-year flow of blood stops his procession. But what about the little girl? Sure enough, word comes that in the delay the daughter has died. Jesus eventually arrives at Jairus' home. He says to Jairus, "Do not *fear*, only *believe*" (5:36). Once again we see these *two* roads open to people in the light of the kingdom-come-near. People can be afraid or they can believe. Jairus believed. Jesus raised his daughter from the dead. The people were amazed. Good soil that yields thirtyfold, sixtyfold and a hundredfold is always amazing!!

The third "good soil" person in this chapter 5 trilogy is the woman with the twelve-year flow of blood. Her hopeless condition is described in detail. Each of the "good soil" people in Mark 5 faces hopelessness. In their desperation they turn to Jesus. Jesus calls their desperate coming to him FAITH. In her desperation the unclean woman touched the hem of his garment, *believing* that if she touched him she would be made whole. And she was. She was made whole in public. This woman, after all, was unclean. She had a *social disease*. She was not to be in the company of other people. But here she is in public and in public she is healed!

When Jesus felt power go forth from himself he wondered aloud about who had touched him. The woman knew that she would have to confess in public and she was *afraid*. But Jesus said to her: "Daughter, your *faith* has made you well; go in peace, and be healed of your disease" (5:34). A woman has *heard* the word of Jesus. A woman of *fear* has become a woman of *faith*. The Sower's seed has fallen upon her life and she has become whole. The seed bore fruit: thirtyfold, sixtyfold and a hundredfold.

Quite in contrast to Jesus' command to the Gerasene to proclaim what Jesus had done for him, this story ends with a call to silence. "He strictly ordered them that no one should know this ..." (5:43). We need to remember here the parables of the kingdom in Mark 4.

99

"For there is nothing hidden, except to be disclosed; nor is anything secret, except to come to light" (Mark 4:22). (See also Mark 9:9.) Whatever else this charge of secrecy means, it is secrecy only for a time. The time of coming to light will come soon enough.

Three "good soil" people. Unlikely people at that. An outsider to outsiders. A Gerasene demoniac. An unclean woman. A ruler of the synagogue. Each came to Jesus in desperation. Each heard the words of the Sower as good news. Each moved from fear to faith. Of such is the kingdom of God!

Homiletical Directions

The first possibility here is to include the story of the Gerasene demoniac with the stories in the gospel text appointed for this week. We have before us probably the most spectacular miracles attributed to Jesus in Mark's Gospel. These miracles take place on both Gentile and Jewish lands. The massive story of casting out legions of demons and the incredible story of the raising from the dead are truly eschatological signs that the kingdom is breaking into time and that it is coming for all the world's peoples. When we put the stories together in this way we will emphasize the "pentecost" character of the church (Acts 2:1-42. Preference is given here to the word "pentecost" rather than the more secular term, "inclusive"). The theme of a kingdom that is for all persons is always relevant. We all harbor corners of thought in our minds which will to exclude people from the reign of God's grace. The pentecostal reality of the Christian Church is a desperately needed message in our age of racism and ethnic cleansing!

A second possibility is to follow Mary Ann Tolbert's intriguing suggestion that the three stories in Mark 5 are illustrative of "good soil" people, a reference to the Parable of the Sower. Last week's story of the disciples who *fear* rather than *believe* might be called to mind briefly as a backdrop for the Mark 5 stories. We see clearly the difference between the "rocky ground" and the "good soil."

Story One for our sermon would be the story of the Gerasene demoniac. It's a wonderful story. (The American Bible Society has a brief video version of this story titled "Out of the Tombs.") Themes of Jesus binding the Strong One as a sign of the kingdom and the inclusion of the Gentiles in the coming kingdom could be touched on briefly. Focus the story on the *fear* that this outsider's outsider must have lived with. *Faith* is not mentioned in this story but faith is a good definition of what this unclean man does. He comes to Jesus out of his desperate need. The seed is sown. He believes what he hears. He is healed.

Story Two can focus on these similar realities in the life of Jairus. He falls at Jesus' feet with a word about his desperate need for help for his daughter who is near death. Jairus certainly believes in the power of the Sower. "Come and lay your hands on her, so that she may be made well, and live," he says to Jesus. Jesus comes. But it's too late. The girl is dead. "No," Jesus says, "she is just sleeping." Jesus says one more thing. "Do not *fear*, only *believe.*" The man believes. Jesus raises the young girl from her sleep of death. The seed is sown and bears much fruit.

Story Three focuses on the story in the middle of the Jairus story. Here, again, focus on the contrasting realities of *fear* (v. 33) and *faith* (v. 34). (You might also comment on how unlikely these three candidates in Mark 5 are as "good soil" people.) The Sower sows the word. The woman hears. She believes. "Daughter, your faith has made you well; go in peace, and be healed of your disease." The seed bears fruit thirtyfold and more!

We can, perhaps, draw our listeners into the reality of this text through this matter of fear. It is interesting how fear and faith are contrasted in Mark's Gospel. Mark doesn't define just what that fear is. It may have manifold expressions. So it does in the life of our hearers. These stories call people of fear to come, in the midst of their desperate need, to the Sower. "The Sower sows the word" (Mark 4:14). We allow that seed to fall on us when we read God's Word and when we hear God's Word in the mouth of those who proclaim and testify.

We bring the "soil" of our lives to the Sower. This is faith. We come believing that the Sower's seed has the power to fructify the "soil" that is our lives. We come believing that the Sower can make things grow in our lives — thirtyfold, sixtyfold and a hundredfold. That's what we do. In faith we just keep on coming to the Sower. There is no magic here. It's not just a matter of coming once and watching the "soil" of our lives break into instant fruit. It is part and parcel of our culture to expect everything to happen instantly! Faith is not necessarily instantaneous. It is a lifelong reality. If we don't see the fruits today, we come back to the Sower tomorrow and the next day. One day, if not this day, we will be "good soil" people. Most certainly the Sower has the power ultimately to bring our fragile human soil out of the grave and make it blossom forth thirtyfold, sixtyfold and a hundredfold in all eternity!

---

1. Mary Ann Tolbert, *Sowing The Gospel* (Minneapolis: Fortress Press, 1989), p. 165.

Chapter 16
Proper 9; Pentecost 8

Mark 6:1-13

Our text for this week records a sudden change of context. Jesus had just been at the home of Jairus, a synagogue ruler, and raised his twelve-year-old girl from death. Now, suddenly, he has come to his own country; he has come to Nazareth. It is not just the scene that shifts. In his own home country people take offense at his very presence. "Where did this man get all this?" the hometown folk wonder aloud. "What is this wisdom that has been given to him?" (Mark 6:2).

This is a striking shift in the story. At the end of Mark 4 the disciples asked a crucial question about Jesus' identity. "Who then is this, that even the wind and the sea obey him?" (Mark 4:41). This question is answered in dramatic form in Mark 5. Mark 5 records the greatest miraculous deeds of Jesus' earthly ministry. He drives out a legion of unclean spirits. He heals a woman with a twelve-year flow of blood. He raises a young woman from the dead. All this and the hometown folks are offended! He was just a carpenter's son, after all. Truly, Jesus could not in his own day, and cannot in our day, prove his identity to people through signs and wonders. If great signs and wonders could do the deed, then everyone would have believed in him then, and now.

Signs and wonders most assuredly did not call the people in Nazareth to faith. In fact, so great was their unbelief that Jesus could not do any mighty work among them except to heal a few sick people. (Remember that Jesus' family also did not understand his true identity: Mark 3:31-35.) Jesus could perform no miracles because of their lack of faith. We are on dangerous theological grounds here. Some commentators assert that Mark's view is that people must have faith or Jesus can do no miracles. Miracles, that is, are the fruit of faith, not the cause of faith. One must hold some kind of predestinarian view to come to this conclusion. How else can we explain why some people have faith *prior to their encounter with Jesus* and other people have not faith? The idea that what Jesus can do in our lives is dependent upon us and our faith is theologically problematic. We wind up questioning our faith whenever something goes awry in our relationship to God. When we do this, faith is often seen as something *we* are responsible for. We must do better. We must manufacture a stronger faith.

We have indicated earlier that faith is born of the Spirit when human beings encounter the story of Jesus. It is the story of Jesus that initiates and calls us to faith! We bring the soil of our lives to the telling of the story. Faith springs to life at this intersection. If faith is not created we come again and again, for the promise is that *God is faithful* to us in and through the story of Jesus. Let us, therefore, not take the occasion of this text to blame our people for their lack of faith, which, in turn, prevents Jesus from doing any mighty work in their lives! The Sower soweth yet!!

In his commentary on Mark, Donald Juel admits that these verses read as if faith is a prerequisite for Jesus' miracles. He cites the exorcism stories in Mark 1:21-28 and 5:1-20 as examples where that is not the case. "How one gets faith — how one comes to understand matters that are contrary to ordinary sense and that Jesus seems intent upon keeping hidden — are questions the narrative has yet to answer." [1]

The hometown folk don't get it. They can't figure out the identity of their local carpenter's son. (Note the questions of identity raised in Mark 6:14-16.) Those who should be the real insiders prove to be outsiders. What kind of "soil" are these people? Are they like the seed sown on the path or seed sown on rocky ground?

Jesus left Nazareth and went on a preaching tour. On tour he called to himself the twelve and sent them out in mission. Are the twelve sent out because they are men of great faith? Hardly. And their hardness of heart will continue to grow! What kind of role models are the twelve anyway? But, in spite of their seeming lack of understanding and fear (Mark 4:40-41), the twelve are sent on a mission to do what Jesus does in his mission. When they return from their sojourn they are called *apostles* for the first and only time in Mark's Gospel (6:30). This is surely a sign of the future.

Jesus is preparing the disciples for their ministry beyond his death. This is clearly an anticipation of the Christian Church and its mission.

The disciples go forth to do what Jesus had been doing. They go forth to proclaim the coming of the reign of God. In Mark's telling of the Jesus story a vital part of the ministry of Jesus in establishing the kingdom is an attack on the world of the demonic. (See 1:21-28, 34, 39; 3:14-15, 20-30; 5:1-20.) Jesus, therefore, gives the twelve authority over the unclean spirits (6:7). In a report of their ministry we hear that they cast out many demons and healed many that were sick (6:13).

The ministry of the twelve will be much like that of Jesus. Some will receive them, some will not (6:10-11). The mystery of faith remains! It is very interesting that Jesus sent his disciples out dependent upon the hospitality of strangers! Missionaries dependent upon the hospitality of strangers. That must also mean that people engaged in mission are called to carry out that mission in a hospitable manner.

Homiletical Directions

The issues raised in Mark 6:1-6 are important faith issues. Our recommendation, therefore, is that these verses of today's two-story text be the focus of preaching. If there is a need in your congregation to focus on the call to mission and the nature of the church, it would be best to center attention on 6:7-13.

Story One of a sermon on Mark 6:1-6 might well begin with a review of Mark 4:35—5:43. How much of a review is necessary will depend upon how much of these stories was shared on the previous pericope text. The purpose of reviewing these stories is to set the context for today's story. The question of Jesus' identity is at stake. The disciples raise the question: "Who then is this, that even the wind and the sea obey him?" (Mark 4:41). Mark 5 provides a stunning answer. Jesus is the One who casts out the devil's legions, heals the sick and raises the dead. In each of these stories the faith of those who encounter Jesus is made explicit. That faith consists most centrally in the fact that they come to Jesus in the midst of their great need. They come to Jesus with open hands. They come

105

to receive.

We have the context for Mark 6:1-6. Who is Jesus? A great worker of miracles! People come to him. When Jesus and the receptive approach of faith meet, amazing things take place. Story Two will pick up today's text. Things looked great for the miracle worker when he was on the road. At home, however, it doesn't go so well. Here is where the insiders live. They know this One. We expect them to believe. They do not believe. They come to Jesus all right, but they come with questions, lots of questions. Their minds are so actively inquisitive that they have no room to receive the gifts Jesus offers. "... He could do no deed of power there, except that he laid his hands on a few sick people and cured them. And he was amazed at their unbelief" (Mark 6:5-6).

This might be a good place to give voice to the questions raised by the people you serve. You know the questions being raised in your community better than anyone else. Put these present-day questions in the mouth of the townsfolk as well. Get the faith issue on the table in its yesterday shape and its today shape. (You might want to include in this telling of today's text as Story Two the examples of the exorcisms which seem to be dependent on Jesus' word alone: Mark 1:21-28; 5:1-20.) Jesus is amazed as much by our contemporary questions as he was by the questions of his kinfolk.

As a conclusion to this sermon we might seek to set up a dialogue between the questions of identity raised yesterday and today — and Jesus' word of promise.

"Where did this man get all this?" Jesus: "I am the Son of God."

"What is the wisdom that has been given to him?" Jesus: "I come with the wisdom of the kingdom of God."

"Who are you for us today anyway?" Jesus: "I am the Sower. I have come to sow the Word."

"What if I just can't believe in you?" Jesus: "I just keep on sowing."

"Where can I turn for assurance?" Jesus: "Read my Word. Listen to my Word. I sow the Word to call you to faith."

"What can I do about you?" Jesus: "Just keep on coming with a receptive heart. You keep coming. I'll keep sowing. I will never give up on you. I'll be sowing the word of life on the soil of your heart for all eternity. Amen."

---

1. Donald H. Juel, *Mark* (Minneapolis: Augsburg, 1990), p. 92.

Mark 6:14-29

Today's text centers in two men: John the Baptist and King Herod. The identity of Jesus is the issue immediately at hand. We discussed this identity issue in the previous chapter, noting that Mark 4:35—6:6 deals with this question. The disciples wonder who Jesus is. Jesus proceeds to demonstrate who he is through a series of spectacular miracles. He drives out a legion of demons, heals a woman with a flow of blood and raises a young girl from the dead. Still, when he arrives in his hometown, his kinfolk could only see that he was a lowly carpenter's son. They were offended by him!

In 6:14ff. we hear that King Herod has heard of Jesus. This occasions a kind of summary of the kinds of answers that were being given to the question of Jesus' identity. Some thought John the Baptist had risen from the dead (6:14). Others thought he was like one of the prophets, Elijah perhaps (6:15). Interestingly enough, the characters in Mark's story never do seem to quite "get it" with Jesus' identity. God declares who Jesus is (1:11; 9:7). The demons know who he is (1:24-25, 34; 3:11-12; 5:7). But very few humans get it. The disciples surely don't get it. Neither do the hometown folk. Neither does King Herod.

Herod thinks this person he has heard about must be John the Baptist, whom he had killed, risen from the dead (6:16). This becomes an occasion for the gospel writer to bring us up to date on the story of John the Baptist. We remember that Jesus' ministry began with the arrest of John the Baptist (Mark 1:14).

The return to John at a time when Jesus seems to be enjoying success and popularity introduces a sobering note into the story again. It serves as a reminder of what happens to preachers who threaten established authorities. The confusion between Jesus and John insinuates that a similar fate awaits Jesus.[1]

108

John precedes Jesus. He is a model of what will happen to Jesus. We might consider this story to be the "passion" story of John the Baptist. John the Baptist's story ends here with his burial by his disciples (6:29). When Jesus died there were no disciples to be found. He had to be buried by a stranger!

In Mary Ann Tolbert's reading of the typology of the Parable of the Sower she views Herod as an example of seed sown among the thorns. Herod and the ruler who comes to Jesus to find out what he must do to inherit eternal life (Mark 10:17-31, appointed for Pentecost 22) are her chief examples in Mark's story of hearers who are like thorny ground. We can probably add the story of Pilate to the thorny ground characters in Mark's Gospel (Mark 15:1-15).

Let's remind ourselves of Jesus' description of the thorny ground people. "And others are those sown among the thorns; these are the ones who hear the word, but the cares of the world, and the lure of wealth, and the desire for other things come in and choke the word, and it yields nothing" (Mark 4:18-19). It is certainly a plausible hypothesis to see Herod as a model of this kind of behavior. Herod had a kind of love/hate relationship with John the Baptist. Herod may have hated John for telling him that it was not lawful for him to have his brother's wife. That was enough for Herodias. "Kill him," she commanded of Herod. Herod couldn't! He feared John the Baptist, knowing that John was a righteous man. So he protected John. But more than protection! Herod called upon John at secret times for spiritual counsel. Herod heard John gladly! The seed had been sown.

Now it came to pass that Herod gave a great birthday banquet. The daughter of Herodias danced. Herod was so overcome with the power of her dance that he offered to give her up to half of his kingdom! That's not what Herodias had in mind, however. She had John the Baptist in mind. "I want you to give me at once the head of John the Baptist on a platter" (6:25). The king was deeply grieved at this request for the head of his spiritual counselor. He was exceedingly sorry. Herod was in a tough spot. He was deeply perplexed. But he sold out! He had made an oath. His guests had heard it. He must keep his word. And so it was that the *cares of the world* choked out the word he had heard. The seed that John had sown yielded nothing!

We must have some genuine sympathy for Herod. He has heard the word. He heard it gladly. But it was choked out by worldly cares. Ministry is lived out in the midst of all kinds of people who fit a similar description. The rich ruler fits the same mold. We have much sympathy for him, too. The disciples were astonished that Jesus could turn this good, good man away. Here was a righteous man. He wanted to inherit eternal life. Jesus loved this man! "You lack one thing," Jesus said to him. "Go, sell what you own, and give the money to the poor ..." (Mark 10:21). The ruler was shocked! He went away sorrowful for he had many possessions. The ruler had heard the word sown; his life had borne much fruit. But in the end the *lure of wealth* choked out the seed that had been sown. His life yielded nothing!

And, Pilate (Mark 15:1-15). Mark paints him, too, as one who is sympathetic to the plight of the Sower. "Do you want me to release for you the King of the Jews?" he pleaded with the crowd (15:9). No! The crowd wanted Barabbas. Pilate knew this was all wrong. It was all jealousy that led the chief priests to try to get rid of this good man. "Then what do you wish me to do with the man you call the King of the Jews?" (15:12). Pilate still hopes to avoid the worst. The crowd rebuffs him again. They want him crucified. "Why," Pilate implores, "what evil has he done?" (15:14). Pilate's pleas went unheeded. The crowd shouted, "Crucify!" "So Pilate, *wishing to satisfy the crowd*, released Barabbas for them; and after flogging Jesus, he handed him over to be crucified" (15:15). Here stood the Sower. Pilate was impressed. But the *desire for other things* choked out the seed that had been sown. Pilate yielded nothing!

Homiletical Directions

We have indicated above that today's text revolves around John the Baptist and King Herod. Our sermon will differ quite radically depending on which of these two men we decide to place stage center. It would be quite difficult to try to include both men because the stories move in different directions. Our suggestion is that the focus be upon King Herod, who gets very little press!

110

The comments above suggest the outline for a sermon which will begin with the story of King Herod. This is to be a sermon which demonstrates what Jesus means by "thorny ground" in his Parable of the Sower. Herod's story can be told as an example of a person in whom the *cares of the world* choke out the word. The rich ruler's story will be told as an example of how the *lure of wealth* chokes out the word. The Pilate story exemplifies how the *desire for other things* (popularity in this case) chokes out the word. You may decide to touch the rich ruler's story lightly in light of the fact that this text (Mark 10:17-31) will be the Gospel story for Pentecost 22. Another possibility, of course, would be to wait until Pentecost 22 to tell these three stories of thorny ground people.

These are easy stories to tell! Some of the main lines for the telling have been suggested above. The dilemmas faced by this trio are extremely relevant to the temptations to present-day persons on whom the Sower's seed has been sown. In the telling of each story it would be well to embellish the central metaphor with contemporary examples. The *cares of the world* choke out the word for King Herod. What kinds of worldly cares choke out the word among people today? How does the *lure of wealth* (rich ruler) manifest itself today? How does the *desire for other things* (Pilate) incarnate itself among us? Weave these present realities into your story telling.

These "thorny ground" stories are extremely relevant for us today. Christians have sold out to the surrounding culture in each of these "thorny ground" ways. This sermon may cut close to the heart of many listeners. So be it!

Tell these three stories. (Two if you do not include the rich ruler.) Weave into the old story contemporary ways in which people are like the "thorny ground" today. Then say "amen" and sit down. The greatest temptation with these stories is to batter people with them and then *moralize* them. We had better change our ways and put the Sower first in our lives or else! No. Your listeners will apply the stories to themselves as they see fit. (The great temptation, of course, is for the hearer to see how these stories fit *other* people. In this case they will really like your sermon. "Great sermon, pastor. You really told *them*!")

Paul Ricoeur once said that "obedience follows the imagination." Stories help to transform the imagination. Let your hearers imagine their way into these stories. Let them imagine themselves in the shoes of King Herod or the rich ruler or Pilate. Let them imagine themselves getting out of those shoes. Let them imagine themselves as *transformed* people. Let them be with these stories.

It is recommended that you close with prayer. The prayer should include an invocation of the Holy Spirit to use these stories to show *each and every one of us* the thorny groundedness of our lives. The prayer should close with a reminder that Jesus did not come to call the righteous, but sinners (Mark 2:17). Jesus, after all, is in the *transformation* business. The One who came to transform sinners into saints can also transform "thorny ground" people into good soil for the gospel.

---

1. Donald H. Juel, *Mark* (Minneapolis: Augsburg, 1990), p. 95.

Mark 6:30-34, 53-56

In her outline of Mark's Gospel, Mary Ann Tolbert presents Mark 6:35—8:21 as a unit of material. The next unit she identifies is 8:22—10:52. She suggests that both units of material can be read as the unfolding of the hardness of the hearts of the disciples. In the section of 6:35—8:21 Jesus feeds the multitudes two times (6:30-44; 8:1-9). Following each feeding story Jesus gets in the boat with his disciples (6:45-52; 8:14-21). (We have looked at these boat stories in chapter 14.) What we see in the flow of these stories is the hardening of the hearts of the disciples (Mark 6:52). The description of the disciples' hearts as being *hardened* fits Tolbert's assignment of the disciples as the *rocky ground* in Mark's version of the Parable of the Sower. (See also 8:17-21.)

Tolbert is convinced on these grounds that the hardening of the hearts of the disciples and the general blindness of the people to the true identity of Jesus begins to make it difficult for Jesus to perform miracles. Where there is no faith, Jesus cannot do the miraculous.

> *As the story of Jesus' rejection by his hometown and consequent inability to accomplish mighty works (6:1-6) makes clear, miracles in the Gospel are not signs to induce faith in unbelievers; they are, instead, the fruits of faith. Since faith is the prerequisite of miracle, as the disciples manifest deeper degrees of unfaith, Jesus encounters greater difficulty in performing mighty works.* [1]

There is some textual evidence for hardness of hearts and fewer miracles, but we would take a false theological turn if we were to accept Tolbert's thesis without reservation. Faith cannot be something that simply pre-exists as the good soil for the gospel.

This seems to imply that faith is a kind of pre-existing human condition that we can *produce by ourselves* as we get ready to hear the gospel. It would be better to say, as has been said earlier, that faith arises at the intersection of the Sower's sown seed and the soil of human hearts. How that happens remains a mystery for us until this very day. We dwell here in the realm of the work of the Holy Spirit.

The text for this Sunday fits precisely the dictionary definition of the word *pericope*: "cutting all around." Today's text "cuts around" Jesus' feeding of the five thousand. The opening verses assigned for today indicate that Jesus had great compassion on the crowd. Jesus, that is, acted like a shepherd to people who were "like sheep without a shepherd." Israel had great traditions of the shepherd. In all three stories of the origin of David he is depicted as a shepherd boy: 1 Samuel 16:6-13 (v. 11); 14-23 (v. 19); 17:1-58 (v. 15). Psalm 23 and Ezekiel 34 present God as the Great Shepherd of Israel.

The assigned text then omits the story of Jesus feeding the Jewish multitude (6:35-44) and the second boat scene of Jesus with his disciples (6:45-52). The text concludes with verses 53-56, which are rather general descriptions of Jesus' ministry. What is omitted here is more important than what is retained! It is unfortunate that the lectionary omits Jesus' first feeding miracle. The lectionary also omits Jesus' second or Gentile feeding of the multitudes in 8:1-9. It is important to Mark to tell two feeding stories. It is important, therefore, for us to include them in our preaching of Mark's Gospel.

Feeding people with bread is a recurrent theme of the Bible's story of God's ways with humans. There are Old Testament stories that can be told in relation to God's feeding ways. In Exodus 16 we read the story of God feeding Israel with manna in the wilderness. There is also a story told about the prophet Elijah providing food for the widow at Zarephath (1 Kings 17:8-16). Donald Juel cites the feeding done by Elisha in 2 Kings 4:42-44 as the most remarkable parallel to Mark's feeding stories. On the one hand, therefore, one can put the feeding miracles in biblical perspective by hearing them in connection with stories from the past.

114

On the other hand, one can put these miracles in perspective by hearing them in connection with the feeding that will follow. Hear Juel:

> *The string of verbs ("took bread ... blessed, broke, and gave") is identical to that in the account of the last meal (14:24). In the account of the feeding of the 4000 that follows in Mark 8:1-9, the sequence of verbs is the same, with the exception of the second, which is "give thanks" instead of "bless"— the former being a term that has a special place in Christian eucharistic practice.* [2]

Commentators generally agree that the feeding story in Mark 6 is a feeding of Jewish people and the feeding of the multitude in Mark 8 is a feeding of Gentiles. After the first feeding miracle Jesus gets in the boat with the disciples and goes "...to the other side, to Bethsaida ..." (6:45). Mark 6:46 places Jesus in Gennesaret. In 7:24 Jesus moves to the region of Tyre and Sidon followed by a stay in the Decapolis, 7:31. Throughout this section, that is, Jesus is in the land of the Gentiles.

There have also been efforts to interpret the differing numbers of leftover loaves as signs of a Jewish and a Gentile feeding. The twelve baskets of leftovers (6:43) would symbolize Israel. There are seven baskets of leftovers in the second feeding (8:8). Some believe that seven is the number that symbolizes the Gentiles. It is a number of wholeness and universality. Other interpreters, however, discount these number theories. It would seem to make ultimate sense that Mark has told these stories to demonstrate that Jesus' ministry is for all people. Given the Old Testament stories that deal with feeding, it is probably not surprising that Mark uses this kind of story to symbolize that Jesus' ministry is, indeed, the "pentecost" of all humanity. There is mission in these stories!

There is also much blindness in these stories. As we have indicated, both feeding stories are followed by boat stories. Boats mean disciples. Boats mean that the disciples don't get it! Re-read those stories! Note, too, the reaction of the Pharisees to the feeding. They watch the feeding and immediately ask for a sign! This is comical when you hear the story told aloud orally. Two great feedings and the Pharisees ask for a sign. Two great feedings and the disciples are worried that they don't have enough to eat. They only have one loaf! (8:14, 16). Jesus' exasperation with the disciples is incredible. He pounds numbers at them. "How many leftovers were there?" They answer dutifully with the numbers but they still don't get it. "Do you have eyes and cannot see?" Jesus pleads. "Do you have ears and cannot hear?" (Remember the similarity to Mark 4:11-13!!) One thing is absolutely clear. For Pharisees and disciples alike, Jesus' great signs of feeding did not lead to faith. What does this mean for us?!

Homiletical Directions

We've put a lot of material together in our comments above which creates a great variety of story possibilities for preaching. Mark has only three stories that deal with bread. Jesus feeds two multitudes with bread and he breaks bread with his disciples on the Passover (Mark 14:22-25). This text, this institution of the Lord's Supper, will be part of a long text on Passion or Palm Sunday (Mark 14:1—15:47). What this normally means is that Mark's stories of Jesus and bread never get told! The lectionary accounts for this by including four Sundays on Jesus and bread from the Gospel of John! Still, *Mark's* story does not get told. This is a Sunday to do so.

Mark's bread stories can be told from one of two quite different perspectives. Story One would be the feeding story in Mark 6:35-44. In the telling of this story we might pick up the theme of manna in the wilderness. The God of the Bible is a God who provides bread for people. ("Give us this day our daily bread.") Bread, of course, is a universal symbol of a deep human need. Jesus provides for that need. Jesus is a Shepherd who takes great care of his flock!

Story Two would be the feeding story in 8:1-9. Set this story in its Gentile context so that the stories told together have about them the universal shape of the church's mission of bread! It will be important in the telling of both feedings to put an accent on the numbers. Those numbers become especially important in light of Jesus' conversation with his disbelieving disciples in 8:14-21.

116

Story Three can be a telling of the institution of the Lord's Supper from Mark 14. An important link between these bread stories is the reality that Jesus is concerned with our whole being. The Lord's Supper stands among us as a symbol that Christ is a Shepherd who feeds us body and spirit. The physicality of the bread in the supper needs to be linked with our need for physical bread. The bread and wine of the supper are symbols of our Shepherd's care for our many hungers. This way of telling these stories puts the emphasis on the *initiative of God* in reaching out to feed hungry people. That is a good gospel-centered reality to fix at the center of your sermon.

Readers of these pages will represent many denominations. Having told these bread stories, you have a wonderful opportunity to say some things about your church's understanding of this sacrament.

The telling of the bread stories in Mark 6 and 8 coupled with the institution of the Lord's Supper in Mark 14 can also focus on *human faith in response* to God's feeding. A first possible way of telling these stories is to put the accent on God's initiative. A second way of telling the stories would put the focus on human response to God's initiative. In the boat with Jesus after the first feeding miracle we discover that the disciples' hearts are *hardened*. After the feeding story in Mark 8 we hear the Pharisees asking for a sign. Somehow they missed the point! We all miss the point at times! And again Jesus gets in the boat with the disciples. He grills them about the numbers. Their hearts continue to be hardened.

The sermon can conclude with speculation about our response to the bread stories. Today it's our turn to be fed at the Shepherd's table. How shall we leave this table? Will our hearts be good soil or rocky ground? Flesh out this challenge to the members of your congregation in a manner that is appropriate to the understanding of faith in your theological tradition.

---

1. Mary Ann Tolbert, *Sowing the Gospel* (Minneapolis: Fortress Press, 1989), p. 180.

2. Donald H. Juel, *Mark* (Minneapolis: Augsburg, 1990), p. 98.

Mark 7:1-8, 14-15, 21-23

With Mark 7 we come to some repetition of basic Markan themes. Mary Ann Tolbert writes: "Since the basic typology is established and identified by Mark 6, Mark 7-10 can develop and amplify the fundamental patterns for the sake of the audience's greater appreciation."[1] The typology to which she refers is that set forth in the Parable of the Sower.

We meet the Pharisees and the scribes from Jerusalem again. We have earlier on identified the Pharisees with the seed sown on the path. The Pharisees hear the word but Satan comes and immediately snatches the word from them. In Mark 2 the Pharisees hear the word along with everyone else. Their response, however, is almost always posited with the question, "Why?" "Why does this fellow speak in this way? It is blasphemy!" (Mark 2:7). "Why does he eat with tax collectors and sinners?" (Mark 2:16). "Why do John's disciples and the disciples of the Pharisees fast, but your disciples do not fast?" (Mark 2:18). "Look, why are they doing what is not lawful on the sabbath?" (Mark 2:24). And now the question is, "Why do your disciples not live according to the traditions of the elders, but eat with defiled hands?" (Mark 7:5). We've met these people before!

The scribes from Jerusalem have also been heard from. It was the scribes from Jerusalem who claimed that Jesus was possessed by Beelzebul (Mark 3:22). Chapter 7 has definite narrative connections to what has gone before.

A second narrative connection for this block of material is the land of the Gentiles. We pointed out in the last chapter that the first feeding of the multitudes is a Jewish feeding. Following this feeding Jesus moves into Gentile country. Immediately prior to the conversation in Mark 7:1-23 Jesus is in Gennesaret among Gentiles.

Immediately following this story Jesus is in Tyre and Sidon (7:24). There Jesus will encounter a Syrophoenician woman.

One of the fundamental issues faced by the early church had to do with eating. Could Gentiles eat with believing Jews? Peter got into deep trouble with the Jerusalem church leaders on this matter. After experiencing a powerful vision that convinced him that there was no such thing as unclean food (Acts 10:9-15), Peter proceeded to *eat* with Cornelius and his household. The church leaders were beside themselves. They said to Peter: "Why did you go to uncircumcised men and eat with them?" (Acts 11:3). A little evangelism is all right. But to eat with such people?? Never!

Werner Kelber is convinced that it is this issue of table fellowship with Gentiles that underlies this story:

> The integration of the Gentiles constitutes a difficult problem for (Mark), which calls for special clarification. Before the acceptance of the Gentiles is formalized, the legal issue has to be settled. This is the function of the abolition of ritual taboos (7:1-23) ... In the context of the Gospel's story line the abolition of the ritual taboos breaks down the legal barrier which had stood in the way of accepting the Gentiles on their terms. What counts in the Kingdom of God is not Jewishness or Gentileness but the heart of the people.[2]

It is interesting to note, in this connection, that three of the "controversy" questions put to Jesus by the Pharisees in Mark 2 have to do with *eating*. Eating is a matter of vital importance in the Jewish religious system. We are not dealing here with a trivial matter. The Pharisaic system sought to *sanctify all areas of life*. "Washing of hands is a mark of respect for every aspect of God's created order."[3] Jesus puts an entire system in jeopardy, therefore, by allowing his disciples to eat with unwashed hands.

The basic argument between Jesus and the Pharisees and the scribes from Jerusalem in Mark 7 is over the right relationship between the *oral* traditions of the elders and the *written* traditions of this people of God. The accusation made to Jesus is that his disciples do not follow the oral tradition of the elders when they eat with unclean hands. Jesus replies to them on the basis of written scripture, quoting the prophet Isaiah. In quoting Isaiah Jesus accuses his accusers of putting oral tradition above written tradition. The laws of oral tradition force people to violate the written tradition! This is precisely the point of the example of "Corban."

Jesus goes on to call into question the whole system of laws about eating. Nothing that enters our body from the outside can do us harm. That means that the whole system of laws about eating is abrogated! For Jesus, purity is a matter of the heart. It is what is inside a person that counts! If the inside, if the heart, is evil — it will produce evil. If the heart is good — it will produce good. The laws of eating have nothing to do with the purity of a person's heart.

A final word on this matter from Juel:

> For Judaism (certainly later rabbinic Judaism and also the perfective of the Pharisees in Mark) the relationship with God and the world is mediated by the Torah, understood as a structure that orders all of life in terms of holiness. For Jesus' followers, the relationship with God and the world is mediated by Jesus, whose desire to heal and save acknowledges no boundaries.[4]

Homiletical Directions

The narrative possibilities with this text are quite limited. The connections we have made above to the Pharisees and the Gentiles offer some promise for story telling and proclamation. In relation to the Pharisees and the scribes of Jerusalem we can reference again the Parable of the Sower. Story One, that is, would remind listeners of hearers who are like seed sown on the path. Satan comes and immediately snatches the word away. Such people do not *hear the new that is offered.* This is the characteristic of the Pharisees in Mark 2. Remind your listeners briefly of the "Why?" questions that were on the lips of the Pharisees. These people are so blinded by their traditions that they cannot see the NEW thing God is doing in Jesus. They fail to see that new wine needs new wineskins! (Mark 2:22). You may want to take up some ways in which we modern people do the same kind of thing. We are so stuck, that is, in our own familiar, traditional, customary forms of religion that we fail to *hear and understand* (Mark 7:14. Remember Mark 4:3, 9).

Story Two would take up the text beginning with another "Why?" question from Pharisees and scribes from Jerusalem: "Why do your disciples not live according to the traditions of the elders, but eat with defiled hands?" (Mark 7:5). This presents us with the opportunity to tell the text as story. The textual story has two aspects. First, we need to lay out this conflict between the traditions of the elders that the Pharisees subscribe to and Jesus' call to ground oneself in the written word of God. Having set that story forth we can come to the second aspect of this text.

The second aspect of the text is about God and the human heart. Nothing that enters our body can affect our heart. We are defiled not by what enters our body but what comes forth from our heart. Once the two aspects of the story are presented we can move towards proclamation. The story in the text leaves us wondering about our hearts. Evil things come forth from human hearts. Verses 21-23 make this absolutely clear! Evil things come forth from *our* hearts as well! The good news is that Jesus promises to give us *bread to eat* that will purify our hearts whether our hands are clean or unclean. The good news is that Jesus intends to pour his new wine into our hearts so that our old hearts will be transformed.

The connection between this aspect of the text and our congregation would be particularly appropriate on a Communion Sunday! On such a Sunday we can close our story telling with the promises of God for human hearts. We speak for Jesus and we say: "Come and eat. Come with hands clean and unclean. Come with hearts that bring forth evil. Here I feed you with my bread. Here I offer you the new wine of the gospel. Here I work to purify your heart. Here I work to create a new heart within you. When you leave this place with hearts transformed, new things will come forth from your heart for the health and healing of humankind."

The second narrative option with this text is to work with the Gentile theme in Mark. Story One can set the stage. Jesus is in Gentile lands here. Material both preceding and following today's text can be used.

121

Story Two can take up the textual story in the light of the Gentile problem. You may wish to refer to the problem of eating with Gentiles in the early church. The Acts 10-11 story exemplifies this problem quite well. In light of the kinds of problems the early church faced, our Markan text appears in new light. Jesus isn't worried about clean hands. Jesus isn't worried about traditions of the elders. Jesus is worried about the human heart. All other boundaries need to be broken down. Jesus comes as a gift to all people, to the Jews first, but also to the Gentiles. There are no barriers to prevent God from touching human hearts in Jesus Christ.

In conclusion we can speak to our people about the new thing that Jesus Christ does for human hearts. "I break down all the barriers that people have erected to exclude some from my kingdom," Jesus says to us today. "I break down all the barriers that religious people have erected to exclude you from my kingdom. I am prepared to meet you heart to heart. Bring your sinful, broken heart to me. I'll give you a heart transplant. I will take your old heart and give you a new one. Then forth from your heart will come all things good."

1. Mary Ann Tolbert, *Sowing The Gospel* (Minneapolis: Fortress Press, 1989), p. 171.

2. Werner H. Kelber, *Mark's Story of Jesus* (Philadelphia: Fortress Press, 1979), pp. 37, 39-40.

3. Donald H. Juel, *Mark* (Minneapolis: Augsburg, 1990), p. 103.

4. *Ibid.*, pp. 106-107.

Mark 7:24-37

Both of the Markan stories appointed for this week take place in the land of the Gentiles. We have pointed out this Gentile ministry of Jesus in earlier chapters. His Gentile ministry will come to a climax in chapter 8 with the feeding of the Gentile multitude. Today's story of the healing of the daughter of a Syrophoenician woman is an incredible symbol of the breaking down of false barriers for the sake of mission. Jesus breaks all kinds of barriers in this story. He breaks down *geographical* barriers by moving into Gentile lands. He breaks down *ethnic* barriers in his dealings with a Greek woman. He breaks down *sexual* barriers as well. It was a radical thing for Jesus to encounter a woman the way he does in this story. The heavens have been opened and God is loose in the world in Jesus Christ breaking down all kinds of barriers!

The Syrophoenician woman is desperate. Like other desperate people in Mark's story she throws herself at Jesus' feet. She comes on behalf of her daughter who is possessed by a demon. Jesus' answer to the woman is one of the most shocking words ever to come forth from his mouth. "Let the children be fed first," Jesus says to the woman, "for it is not fair to take the children's food and give it to the dogs" (Mark 7:27). Biblical commentators have tried to find any way possible around the harshness of these words. But the words stand. Jesus clearly sees his ministry as a ministry to the children (people of Israel) first and only later to the dogs (Gentiles). Saint Paul says the same thing about his ministry. The gospel, he writes, "... is the power of God for salvation to everyone who has faith, to the Jew first and also to the Greek" (Romans 1:16).

The woman is not put off by Jesus' rebuke. She comes right back at him. "Sir, even the dogs under the table eat the children's crumbs" (Mark 7:28). It is almost as if this foreign woman is giving Jesus a theology lesson! This is certainly the most striking feature of this story. A Gentile woman teaches Jesus. If nothing else this story should remove from us any form of missional arrogance. People whom we encounter with the gospel may also have things to teach us! They are not necessarily strangers to God after all. As Paul said of the Gentiles, "They show that what the law requires is written on their hearts ..." (Romans 2:15).

Finally, this woman is revealed to us as a woman of faith. Because of *her faith* (!), Jesus announces that the demon has left her daughter! This unnamed woman is good soil for the seed of the Gospel. That seed has sprung up within her and produced thirtyfold, sixtyfold and a hundredfold.

The Syrophoenician woman is one of the "little people" in Mark's Gospel who are presented to us as people of faith. These "little people" in Mark's story have "... consistent traits which they share in common: a childlike, often persistent, faith; a disregard for personal status and power; and a capacity for sacrificial service ... they are the 'little ones who have faith.' " [1]

While still in the land of the Gentiles, "they brought to him a deaf man who had an impediment in his speech; and they begged him to lay his hand on him" (Mark 7:32). The Syrophoenician woman *brought her daughter* to Jesus. Some unnamed persons *bring a man* with a speech impediment to Jesus. There are other instances in Mark's Gospel where unidentified persons bring someone to Jesus to be cured. (See for example Mark 2:1-12 and 8:22-26.) "The stories demonstrate the results of faith, though it is not the faith of the sick that is the focus of attention."[2]

Mark is teaching us something here about the *communal nature* of faith. We normally talk about the faith of individuals. The Bible wants us also to be cognizant of the communal nature of faith. The practice of infant baptism clearly underscores the communal nature of faith. One premise of the practice of baptizing infants is the assumption that this child is reborn through the prayers and faith of the community. This is a hard word for us to hear at times in our world which is so individualistic in nature. The Bible challenges our individualism in general, and any purely individualistic notion of "faith" in particular!

124

In both of these stories Jesus heals with the power of the word. "The demon has left your daughter!" says Jesus, and it is so! (Mark 7:29). " 'Ephphatha ... Be opened,' Jesus said, "and immediately his ears were opened, his tongue was released and he spoke plainly" (Mark 7:34-35). These are proclamatory words of Jesus. You may wish to consider structuring your sermon on these stories in such a way that the congregation hears Jesus' words of proclamation and healing as words spoken to them!

The stories end in astonishment. "They were astounded beyond measure, saying, 'He has done everything well; he even makes the deaf to hear and the mute to speak' " (Mark 7:37). This verse reminds us of Mark 2:12: "... they were all amazed and glorified God, saying, 'We have never seen anything like this!' " The stories in Mark 8 are variations on a theme. Jesus comes bringing the kingdom near. One of the human realities that occurs in light of the kingdom's proximity is that human lives are restored to wholeness. These stories of wholeness demonstrate the reality that some soil is good soil which produces thirty, sixty and a hundredfold.

Homiletical Directions

The first preaching possibility we will look at with reference to these stories is a sermon that focuses on Mark's *unnamed women of faith.* They are quite something special — special in a world that thought them to be so non-special that they are not even named! Tell first the story of the unnamed woman in Mark 5:24b-34. This is the woman with a flow of blood that lasted for twelve years. She was desperate. But she knew something special. She believed that all she had to do was touch the hem of Jesus' garment and she would be healed. She touched! "Immediately her hemorrhage stopped; and she felt in her body that she was healed of her disease" (Mark 5:30).

We have looked at this woman's story before. It is part of that great "good soil" chapter: Mark 5. She is one of the first "good soil" people we hear about in the Gospel. She is an unnamed woman with unusual insight into the ministry of Jesus.

Story Two would be the story of the Syrophoenician woman. She, too, is unnamed. She has grasped the nature of Jesus' ministry

125

so well that she proceeds to teach him that he ought to be reaching out to the Gentiles. This aspect of the story is simply incredible. An unnamed woman teaches Jesus!

Story Three could be that of the unnamed woman in Mark 14:3-9. Like the Syrophoenician woman, she has special insight, it seems, into the nature of Jesus' ministry. This story, each of these unnamed-women stories, stands in such clear contrast to the disciples who never understand anything!

When we come to Mark 8 we will begin to deal with the clearest stories of disciples who don't get it. Jesus will tell them three times that he must go to Jerusalem to suffer many things, be rejected, killed and raised to new life (Mark 8:31; 9:30-32; 10:32-34). Jesus reveals to his disciples the world of suffering that awaits his ministry. He calls upon them to take up their cross and follow him into suffering (Mark 8:34-38). But the disciples never get the point! They keep seeing "glory" as their destiny (Mark 9:34; 10:35-37. We will take up this series of passages in more detail in subsequent chapters).

Returning to the story in Mark 14 we understand that Jesus is on the way to Jerusalem to die. The disciples don't get it. An unnamed woman, however, does get it! She breaks open an alabaster jar of ointment and pours it over Jesus' head. People are indignant with this woman. Jesus steps in to rescue the woman and to say of her deed: "… she has anointed my body beforehand for its burial. Truly I tell you, wherever the good news is proclaimed in the whole world, what she has done will be told in remembrance of her" (Mark 14:8-9). This unnamed woman has grasped the nature of Jesus' journey to the cross. She has anointed him for burial. She is most certainly a good-soil woman, a woman of great faith!

The irony of her story, of course, is that the story that will be told in remembrance of her is a story that *does not remember her name*! She is simply one of the "little people" in Mark's Gospel who evidence great faith. The unnamed status of women will end with the coming of the Christian community. In Baptism women are named! Christian Baptism is the only initiation rite in all of the world's religions that is the same for men and women! Women shall be no more unnamed among us.

Having told these three stories of unnamed women of great faith and insight, we might speak of the reality among us today that we don't always know who the *good-soil* people are. We don't know how the Gospel seed is taking root in people. Therefore, in the Christian community, we must treat all people with dignity. We honor all people in our community by using their name. There are "little people" of faith among us today. (Note Mark 9:33-37 on treatment of children!) Jesus calls upon us to *listen* to the "little people." The way of life in the Christian community (listening to the little people) is about as far removed from life in our secular world as it can be.

A second possibility for story telling this week is to focus our attention on the communal aspect of faith. A Syrophoenician woman brings a daughter to Jesus, and he heals the daughter in light of the woman's faith. In Mark 7:31-37 friends bring a man who is deaf and has a speech impediment to Jesus. Jesus heals the man in the light of the faith of the man's community! This is Story One. Story Two can tell again, from this communal faith perspective, the story of the paralytic (Mark 2:1-12). Verse 5 of this story says specifically: "When Jesus saw *their* faith, he said to the paralytic ... ." A third story of this nature is told in Mark 8:22-26. Here people bring a man with a speech impediment to Jesus begging Jesus to touch him and heal him. Jesus responds to *their* faith and heals the man.

These stories reveal to us that faith has a communal nature. This does not mean that faith has no individual nature. We are faced with one of many biblical paradoxes here. Both realities are true. One might emphasize at the conclusion of these stories that we need to be aware of both aspects of faith. The church gathered is a community of faithful people. When our *individual faith is strong* we need to be part of the gathered community to lend strength to others. (There are times when we might feel like we, individually, don't *need* to go to church. The community of people gathered, however, needs us most of all when we are strong.) On the other hand, when our *individual faith is weak*, we turn to the faith of the community to support us. Such is the nature of life in the community of the faithful.

127

Some comments about the way both communal faith and individual faith are present in the Sacrament of Holy Baptism might also be touched upon at this point in the sermon.

---

1. David Rhoads and Donald Michie, *Mark As Story* (Philadelphia: Fortress Press, 1982), p. 130.

2. Donald H. Juel, *Mark* (Minneapolis: Augsburg, 1990), p. 109.

Mark 8:31-38, Mark 8:27-38

We will treat these texts as one. In examining them we have entered what many commentators believe is the central section of Mark's story: 8:22—10:52. The immediate context for this central section of material is the climax of the section that precedes it: Mark 6:35—8:21. We need to say a few words about 8:1-21, as it is omitted from the lectionary. Mark 8:1-9 is the story of the Gentile feeding of the multitude with bread which we have discussed in an earlier chapter. The response to Jesus' feeding of this second multitude is ironic and filled with comedy. The Pharisees ask Jesus for a sign!! Jesus has just fed a second multitude with leftovers abundant and the Pharisees ask for a sign! How blind can they be? They have eyes, but they do not seem to be able to see! Such is Mark's description of *outsiders* (Mark 4:11-12).

The disciples then enter the picture. Their response to Jesus' feeding the multitudes is even more ironic, filled with even greater comedy. They are with Jesus in the boat and they only have one loaf of bread. How can they all eat when there is only one loaf? They've seen Jesus do bread miracles but they have not believed what they have seen. Their eyes, too, are blind. We seem to have reached a climax here in terms of the blindness of the "rocky ground" disciples. Jesus bores in on them with his questions. "Why are you talking about having no bread?" he scolds. "Do you still not perceive or understand? Are your hearts hardened? (Rocky ground!) Do you have eyes, and fail to see? Do you have ears, and fail to hear?" (Mark 8:17-18). It would appear that the disciples who were called *insiders* in Mark 4:11-12 are now *outsiders*. They are the ones who see and do not perceive! They are the ones who hear and do not understand!

This climactic story of hard-hearted, rocky ground disciples sets the stage for the central section of Mark's Gospel (8:22—10:52).

129

The motif of this section is "on the way." Jesus is "on the way" to Jerusalem (Mark 8:27; 9:33-34; 10:32). While "on the way" to Jerusalem Jesus seeks to reveal the truth of his Messianic identity to the disciples. Jesus tries to open their eyes. This whole section of Mark's Gospel is framed by stories in which Jesus opens blind eyes. It begins with the story of the opening of the eyes of a blind man in Bethsaida (8:22-26) and it closes with the opening of the eyes of blind Bartimaeus (10:46-52). Bartimaeus sees and immediately follows Jesus "on the way." He is clearly a *good soil* man! But Jesus cannot open the blind eyes of the disciples! Jesus gives sight to blind men; he cannot, however, break through the blindness of his disciples.

We come to the text of Peter's "confession." Donald Juel says that Peter's confession is the first small sign that the disciples' eyes might be opening. From v. 1 of Mark's Gospel we as readers have known that Jesus' identity is that of Christ/Messiah. Peter's "confession" is the first time in the story that anyone seems to have grasped that identity. Mary Ann Tolbert considers this "confession" of Peter to be the *turning point* of Mark's story. These verses stand at the physical center of the story and they begin to move us toward a revelation of the true identity of Jesus the Messiah.

Werner Kelber states in the strongest terms, however, that Peter's "confession" is a false confession.

> *... The correctness of Peter's so-called confession can only be maintained if one stops reading at this point ... Whatever Peter's concept of Christ, it is in conflict with Jesus' concept of Christ ... Mark sets it up in such a way that the reader almost instinctively identifies with Peter and his Christ confession. He teases the reader, as it were, into accepting Peter's confession at face value. But then Mark unfolds the drama by emphasizing increasingly the negative aspects of Peter until in the end he shatters the veracity of Peter's confession and wrecks the reader's identification with Peter. The scene culminates in the highly dramatic confrontation between Peter and Jesus, each rebuking the other and Peter in the end being exposed as Satan. In the Gospel Peter is the only human being*

130

who is identified, and identified by Jesus, as a satanic person. It is overwhelmingly clear: Peter's confession has not been the correct confession.[1]

Following immediately upon Peter's confession is Jesus' first "passion/resurrection" prediction. (See also 9:30-31; 10:32-34.) Jesus reveals that the Messiah must suffer many things, be killed, and be raised on the third day. This is simply too much for Peter. He obviously cannot comprehend a suffering Messiah. The tension of Mark's story lies in the reality that Jesus is simply not the kind of Messiah that people expected. Messianic expectations were expectations of *glory*. Dreams of glory and power must have danced in Peter's head when he made his "confession." But he had it all wrong. The Messiah is the One who suffers.

This contrast between glory and suffering is played out in Mark's Gospel in a very systematic way. In 8:31 Jesus announces for the first time that he must suffer. This earns Jesus a rebuke from Peter which, in turn, earns Peter a rebuke from Jesus. "Get behind me, Satan!" What a powerful rebuke this is! Peter has clearly not understood what it means to be Messiah. Peter dreams of glory. When it's time to go the mountain of Transfiguration with Jesus, Peter basks in the glory and pleads that it might continue. Peter says to Jesus: " 'Rabbi, it is good for us to be here; let us make three dwellings, one for you, one for Moses, and one for Elijah.' He did not know what to say, for they were *terrified*" (Mark 9:5-6). Terrified. Afraid. Once again the disciples appear as men of fear rather than faith. In their fear-filled lack of faith they long for glory.

"On the way" to Jerusalem Jesus makes a second "passion/ resurrection" prediction. "The Son of Man is to be betrayed into human hands, and they will kill him, and three days after being killed, he will rise again" (Mark 9:31. Mark 9:30-37 is appointed for Pentecost 19). Once again the disciples are afraid. They do not understand. They have eyes but they do not see. They move on to Capernaum and their minds are on glory, not cross! After arriving in Capernaum Jesus asks his disciples what they were arguing about along the way. They are silent. They don't want to admit that they

131

were talking about which of them was the *greatest*. They have ears to hear but they do not hear! Jesus speaks of cross; they speak of glory.

Once more, this time approaching Jerusalem, Jesus reveals his identity. "... The Son of Man will be handed over to the chief priests and the scribes, and they will condemn him to death; then they will hand him over to the Gentiles; they will mock him, and spit upon him, and flog him, and kill him; and after three days he will rise again" (Mark 10:33-34). Jesus speaks of the cross. The disciples stay fixed on glory. James and John ask him if they can sit one at his right hand and one at his left, in glory. (They did not know that the right and left hand were reserved for a couple of criminals and that the place for such honor was the cross [Mark 15:27].) Jesus speaks of the cross. The disciples dream of glory. How difficult it is to grasp the reality that Israel's long-awaited Messiah is to be a suffering Messiah.

Not surprisingly, the call to follow "on the way" with Jesus is a call to a cruciform life (Mark 8:34-38). Kelber explicates this very well:

> *It may be the single most important message the author wishes to convey: there is no life without death, and no Easter without crucifixion. The Markan emphasis lies heavily on the period of suffering and the crucifixion. He does not focus on Easter itself ... The resurrected Jesus, we shall see, never makes an appearance in the Gospel of Mark ... Discipleship is not derived from the glorified Jesus ... For Mark, to be a Christian means to follow Jesus on his way; to drink the cup of suffering; to be concerned with the salvation of others, and less — if at all — with one's own life and well-being.[2]*

Homiletical Directions

There are a great many preaching possibilities for these two Sundays. During Lent it would be well to put the emphasis on Jesus' revelation of his Messianic identity as an identity of suffering. Such a sermon might well begin with the story of Peter's "confession." Peter has it right in principle. Truly Jesus is the Christ.

But he has it wrong in content. Peter thinks of messianic glory. Peter's "confession" sets the stage for Jesus' self-revelation.

Tell next the three stories in which Jesus reveals his true identity: Mark 8:31; 9:30-31; 10:32-34. The focus of these stories will be on the *necessity* of Jesus as a suffering Christ. This is who Jesus is! Revealed to us through these stories is a God who says in effect: "I am God revealed in Jesus. I am a God who must suffer. I suffer in order to share in your sufferings. I identify with you when you suffer. I will walk with you when you suffer and raise you on the third day. I will walk with you in your trials and bring you to new life. I will die with you when you die and bring you with me to eternal life."

A second possibility is to use the entire section of Mark 8:21— 10:52 as a source for stories. Story One would briefly give the context of the blindness of the disciples (Mark 8:14-21) leading to the two healings of blind men: Mark 8:22-26; 10:46-52. Jesus Christ has come to open our eyes!

The disciples, however, have eyes that do not see and ears that do not hear. Tell the story of the three "passion/resurrection" predictions this time from the point of view of the blindness of the disciples. They hear but they do not understand. They hear Jesus speak of cross and they return to glory again and again. The key glory verses are: Mark 9:5; 9:33-37; 10:35-45.

Glory thinking is a fundamental hallmark of much of American Christianity. The American "gospel" is that *if* you truly believe in Jesus, *then* all of your needs will be met. Nothing can stand in your way. To be a Christian is to be bound for glory. This American glory thinking stands in stark contrast to Mark's cross thinking. Our eyes still seem blind to the heart of Jesus' message.

Story telling touching these realities can conclude with a reference to the fact that it is Jesus' intention to open our blind eyes in order that we might see him as the suffering, crucified Messiah. This story telling route can end in one of two ways. We can conclude by "speaking for God." Jesus' word to us today through these stories is, "I have come to open blind eyes. I have come to open your eyes. Hear me proclaim to you the necessity of my suffering. Hear me proclaim to you the inevitability of my death on the cross. Hear my story again and again. When you hear this story told I will be there to open your blind eyes. When you hear this story I will be there to call you to faith in my way of the cross. When you hear this story I will invite you to take up your cross and follow me."

Or this series of stories focused on the blindness of the disciples could end in prayer. Fashion a closing prayer that invites Jesus to open our blind eyes.

Still another route for a sermon on today's texts would focus on Jesus' call to take up his cross and follow (Mark 8:34-38). Here, too, we might tell the stories of Jesus' three "passion/resurrection" predictions along with the disciples' response: they choose the glory road. The structure for this sermon might be as follows: tell the entire text as a story. Make it clear in the telling that you want to highlight Jesus' call to self-denial and cross-bearing. Contrast Peter's confidence in his confession and Jesus' rebuke. Secondly, tell the stories of each "passion/resurrection" prediction along with the disciples' responses of glory thinking. Let Peter's response to Jesus' self-revelation be his wish to build booths on the mountain of transfiguration. Such is Peter's response to Jesus. At this point use as a refrain Jesus' word about taking up the cross. It would go like this. Peter says: "Let's build three booths and stay here." Jesus responds: "If any want to become my followers, let them deny themselves and take up their cross and follow me."

Move then to the second story of the disciples' response. The disciples say: "Which one of us is the greatest?" Jesus says: "If any want to become my followers ...."

Finally, tell the third story of the disciples' response. The disciples say: "Can we sit on your right and left hand in glory?" Jesus says: "If any want to become my followers ...."

You can end your sermon with these challenging words of Jesus ringing in the ears of your hearers. You may determine, however, that the eyes and ears of the disciples you preach to are no better than the eyes and ears of Jesus' disciples. In that case, ending your sermon with an open challenge won't get you or your hearers very far. It will be better to end the sermon with a prayer or a proclamation that calls forth the power of Jesus to lead us from fear to faith, from glory to cross. Open our eyes, Lord. Let us see!

---

1. Werner H. Kelber, *Mark's Story of Jesus* (Philadelphia: Fortress Press, 1979), pp. 47-48.

2. *Ibid.*, p. 52.

Chapter 22
Transfiguration (Last Sunday After The Epiphany)

Mark 9:2-9

The Markan text appointed for these Sundays stands at the very heart of Mark's Gospel. Werner Kelber puts the significance of this story very well:

> *In a number of ways this transfiguration of Jesus (9:2-8) forms the central scene of this whole Gospel. Structurally, in terms of number of verses, it stands almost exactly at midpoint in the gospel story. It constitutes the only "high mountain" scene in the Gospel. Outside of baptism this is the only time the life of Jesus is marked by divine intervention in visible and audible terms ... The literary critic will call this transfiguration story the **scene of recognition**. At one point in a novel or drama or movie the author lets the reader or viewer have a glimpse of the protagonist's full identity, intimating thereby the final outcome of the story. The transfiguration (not Peter's so-called confession!) is this scene of recognition. For a brief moment Jesus is revealed to the three witnesses as the Son of God in full glory.* [1]

The narrative connections for this story are numerous. The other passages in Mark's Gospel where Jesus is revealed to be Son of God form a narrative whole with this passage. Mark 1:1 announces immediately that Jesus is "the Son of God." The baptismal story stands at the outset of Jesus' ministry. This is the first story in which God speaks and identifies Jesus as "my beloved Son" (Mark 1:9-11). The demons seem always to know that Jesus is Son of God (Mark 1:24; 3:11; 5:7). Jesus tells the parable that is the plot synopsis of chapters 11-16 in which he clearly alludes to himself as the "beloved son" (Mark 12:1-11 [vv. 6-7]). Finally and climactically, the Roman Centurion confesses that Jesus is Son of

God (Mark 15:39). The revelation that Jesus is the Son of God stands at the very heart of Mark's narrative. (Psalm 2:7 and 2 Samuel 7:8-17 [v. 14] are Old Testament passages which form a background for this Son of God theme.)

Narrative connections can also be made between this story and the stories of Moses and Elijah in the Old Testament. There are similarities, for example, between this theophany and the Mount Sinai theophany of God to Moses. (See Exodus 24:15-18.) Elijah was also granted a theophany of God on Mount Horeb (1 Kings 19:4-18). It is not surprising, therefore, that it is Moses and Elijah, men who have been to the mountain with God, who appear now on the mountain with Jesus. Moses and Elijah also stand figuratively for the presence of the Law and the Prophets of the Old Testament. When Jesus stands transfigured in the presence of Moses and Elijah he is seen to be the One who fulfills the Law and the Prophets.

And then there are the disciples! They have eyes but they do not see. They have ears but they do not hear. Peter's initial response is to grab for the glory. "It is good for us to be here," Peter says. "Let us make three dwellings, one for you, one for Moses and one for Elijah" (9:5). Jesus is revealing a foretaste of his glory to the disciples. They want to live in this foretaste! They want to capture it and bottle it while they can. "They desire a shortcut to the Kingdom of God by eliminating the dimension of suffering and death ... The glory of transfiguration will not be consummated except through the agony on the cross."[2]

In the flow of Mark's Gospel Jesus has just revealed himself to the disciples for the first time as a Messiah who must suffer (Mark 8:31). Peter rebuked Jesus for such thinking! Then Jesus rebuked Peter: "Get behind me, Satan!" Jesus proceeded to reveal to Peter and the disciples that following him meant the adoption of a cruciform life. We can be sure that Peter didn't like what he was hearing. When he and the disciples thought of Jesus as the Christ they dreamed thoughts of glory and power rather than thoughts of suffering and death. The transfiguration experience is more like it — more in the nature of what they expected. Jesus had told the disciples to prepare for a cruciform life. The first chance they get, however, they grasp for the glory. The stories in 9:30-37 and 10:32-

45 are further examples of the disciples' grab for glory when Jesus wills to speak of the cross. (This theme is developed more fully in chapter 21.) Mark explicates the disciples' lack of understanding a bit further. He tells us that Peter didn't know what to say for he was exceedingly *afraid* (Mark 9:6). The first time that Mark develops this motif of "fear rather than faith" is in the story that follows the Parable of the Sower (Mark 4:35-41). The disciples are in a boat when a great storm arises. They awake Jesus and he stills the storm. But Jesus is puzzled by the attitude of the disciples. "Why are you afraid?" he asks them. "Have you still no faith?" (Mark 4:41). This is the first passage in Mark where the contrast between faith and fear is in evidence. Mark holds these two possibilities of response to Jesus before us here and in many other passages as well. (This theme is developed more fully in chapter 14.)

Further narrative connections can be made with the *booths* (v. 5) and the *cloud* (v. 7). The people of Israel had an annual celebration of the Feast of Booths. This was a major pilgrimage festival in the Jewish year. (See Deuteronomy 16:13-15.) The possible connection of booths in Mark 9 and Deuteronomy 16 is not very clear. Future biblical scholarship may help us on this point. There is a passage in Zechariah 14:16-19 about an eschatological festival of booths. It would appear from this Zechariah passage that this festival could be connected with that which was to come.

The cloud, on the other hand, is a rather consistent Old Testament image for the presence of God. The cloud appeared over both Moses and Elijah in their theophany experiences with God on Mount Sinai.

The voice that identifies Jesus as Son of God also commands the disciples, and us, to *listen* to him! (Mark 9:7). This is a fitting command for a Gospel that presents Jesus as the Sower who spreads the *word* (Mark 4:1-20 [vv. 3, 9, 14]). Jesus invites people to *listen*! In Mark's Gospel listening is more important than seeing.

> *... it is the word, not the image, that brings the kingdom of God in power ... Thus the response of the disciples to the transfiguration in the person of Peter is doubly damning, for not only do they fear what they see ... they*

are impressed by the glorified image after rejecting the
saving words ... The kingdom of God coming in power is
not the result of seeing Jesus' shining garments or his
communion with Elijah and Moses; it is the result of
hearing his word and responding in faith.[3]

Homiletical Directions

Narrative sermons can be forged around many of the themes we have developed above. Most certainly we could tell the Old Testament theophanies of Moses and Elijah as a background for today's story. The emphasis in such a sermon would be on fulfillment. Jesus is the fulfillment of all that is contained in the Law and Prophets. The Law called God's people to obedience. The Prophets called upon God's people to expect One to come in the future who would turn their despair to hope. Jesus is God's new obedience on our behalf. He has come to live within us in order to *transfigure* us into obedient creatures. Jesus is also that One to whom the prophets bore witness. In these end of days Jesus has come to *transfigure* all our hopes and expectations into fulfillment in him.

A sermon might also be built around the lack of faith and understanding on the part of the disciples. We would need to connect this story of the disciples' *fear* with the other passages in Mark which evidence the fear of the disciples. Hardness of heart (the disciples are the "rocky ground" in the Parable of the Sower) characterizes these insiders that Jesus has chosen. They do not see. They do not understand. Their hearts are hardened. Mark's depiction of the role of the disciples as insiders-become-outsiders forms a deep word of caution and alert to those who claim to be the insiders in any age!

This passage is so central to the heart of Mark's message that a sermon on the Son of God theme seems most natural. Story One could tell the story of Mark 1. The Son of God theme is set in motion from the outset of the Gospel. Story Two might concentrate on the three passages where the demons, at least, have understood the presence of the Son of God (Mark 1:24; 3:11; 5:7). The story of the Roman Centurion who climactically confesses that Jesus is Son of God at the foot of the cross (Mark 15:39) might also be told.

These stories form the backdrop for today's story. Tell it now with a focus on the voice of God. Here, as in Mark 1:11, God's voice announces that Jesus is the beloved Son. The command here is to *listen to him*! This command to listen would certainly appear to make the most sense when it is combined with the Parable of the Sower. The Son of God, according to Mark, is the Sower who sows the word. There is good news in this message. The good news is that we can listen as well as anyone in the days that Jesus lived. We can't go to the mountain of transfiguration with the disciples, but we *can listen*!

The Son of God calls us to listen! This call to listen is particularly important in the light of the reality that the disciples who were his closest insiders became outsiders. They listened. They had ears to hear but they did not understand. How do we prevent that from happening to us? By listening over and over and over again. God's Son is a generous Sower who will sow his word until our eyes see and our hearts perceive.

When we listen we hear some wonderful news. When we listen to the story as Mark tells it we hear Jesus say: "I am the Son of God. I am the Son of God come as a Sower to sow God's word in your life. I sow God's word when I cast out demons. I sow God's word when I bring you health. I sow God's word when I announce to you that your sins are forgiven."

There is some darker news from Jesus which we can also receive as good! Jesus, the Sower, says: "I am a Son who 'must undergo great suffering, and be rejected by the elders, the chief priests, and the scribes, and be killed, and after three days rise again' " (Mark 8:31). (This word from Jesus is an important part of the context of today's text. Jesus will repeat this word twice more: 9:30-31; 10:32-34.) "I am a Son who shares your suffering. I am a Son who enters your pain. I am a Son who will ultimately triumph over suffering and death and raise you to life eternal." Listen to him!

---

1. Werner H. Kelber, *Mark's Story of Jesus* (Philadelphia: Fortress Press, 1979), p. 53-54.

2. *Ibid.*, p. 55.

3. Mary Ann Tolbert, *Sowing The Gospel* (Minneapolis: Fortress Press, 1989), p. 207.

Mark 9:30-37

The lectionary moves directly from the story on the Mount of Transfiguration (9:1-8) to Jesus' second "passion/resurrection" prediction (9:30-37). In the intervening passages we see the fear and unbelief of the disciples clearly portrayed. Peter, James and John come down from the mountain with Jesus. They have failed to understand what Jesus means by the "rising of the dead" (Mark 9:10). These are precisely the same disciples who were with Jesus when he raised a twelve-year-old girl from death (Mark 5:35-43). These are the disciples who have just come down from the mountain where the dead were alive! Moses and Elijah were there with them. Still, they fail to understand.

Meanwhile, back on earth, the other disciples have failed in their efforts to drive an evil spirit from a young lad. Jesus is appalled by their *faithlessness*! "You *faithless* generation, how much longer must I be among you?" (Mark 9:19). In our text for today the disciples continue to manifest a lack of faith. They are *afraid* (Mark 9:32).

We have pointed out in earlier chapters how Mark paints these opposing responses to Jesus' person and message. Some are afraid. Some have faith. The story told in Mark 9:14-29 paints a more subtle picture of the relation of faith and fear, of faith and unfaith. The father begs Jesus to cast the demon from his son. "... If you are able to do anything, have pity on us and help us," the father pleads (Mark 9:22). Jesus is indignant at this suggestion. "If you are able!" he shouts back. "Of course I am able." "All things can be done for the one who believes" (Mark 9:23). The father responds in desperation. "I believe," he says, "help my unbelief!" (Mark 9:24). There is more nuance in Mark's story telling here than in the many other Markan stories where faith and unbelief are starkly opposed realities. Faith and unbelief live in all of us *at the same*

142

time. Surely this paradoxical thought comes closer to the reality of our heart's response to Jesus than does a simple either/or.

Today's text contains the second of Jesus' "passion/resurrection" predictions. We have discussed these three predictions (8:30; 9:30-31; 10:32-34) in chapter 21. We saw in these "passion/resurrection" predictions that the disciples much preferred talk of glory to talk of the cross. That is certainly the case in today's reading. The disciples *do not understand* what Jesus is talking about. They are *afraid* (Mark 9:32). Immediately following this second encounter with Jesus' hard words about what is to come to pass in Jerusalem, Jesus and the disciples head for Capernaum. Along the way the disciples' heads are filled with thoughts of glory. "... On the way they had argued with one another who was the greatest" (Mark 9:34). The contrast between cross and glory could hardly be put more starkly.

In chapter 21 the three "passion/resurrection" predictions were discussed together. Here we might move from this story of the disciples' lack of faith and understanding (rocky ground disciples) to the story of their final days with Jesus as told in Mark 14. Mark 14:1—15:47 is the text for the Sunday of the Passion. Only rarely do we take the opportunity afforded by this larger text to discuss the behavior of the disciples in the last days. This Sunday is as good a time as any to link their behavior in Gethsemane and the trial to their rocky-grounded behavior as clearly portrayed by Mark in the first part of his Gospel.

The first clue to what is coming in Mark 14 is the note that Judas Iscariot went to the chief priests in order to betray Jesus (14:10). Mark 14:17-21 tells the actual story of the betrayal. Jesus says to his disciples as they are gathered for the Passover Meal: "Truly I tell you, one of you will betray me, one who is eating with me." The surprising reaction of the disciples as a collective group is their response to him and to the others: "Surely, not I?" None of them is sure that he won't be the man. That's an honest response from men with hardened hearts!

After the meal had ended and they had sung a hymn they went together to the Mount of Olives. There Jesus said to them: "You will all become deserters" (Mark 14:27). Other translations read, "You will all *fall away*." Remember Jesus' explanation for the seed sown on rocky ground, "... they have no root ... when trouble or persecution arises on account of the word, immediately they *fall away*" (Mark 4:17). These words of Jesus in the Parable of the Sower appear to come true in the Garden of Gethsemane.

The Gethsemane story is familiar to us. (See Mark 14:32-42.) Jesus asks the disciples to watch with him while he agonizes in prayer over his destiny. But the disciples fall asleep! Three times! Three times in the boat they failed to grasp what Jesus was all about. Three times in the light of Jesus' "passion/resurrection" predictions which hold forth the cross as central to his destiny we find the disciples bent on glory. Three times they fall asleep. Three times will Peter deny his Lord as Jesus has foretold (Mark 14:29-31, 66-72). Nevertheless! Nevertheless, the Risen Jesus sends word for Peter and the others to meet him in Galilee as he had promised. (See Mark 14:28; 16:7.)

The concluding verses of today's text show Jesus in dialogue with the disciples concerning their "glory thinking," i.e., which one of them is the greatest. "Whoever wants to be first must be last of all and servant of all" (Mark 9:35). Jesus goes on to say to them that the kingdom of God is about welcoming children.

> *In ancient culture, children had no status. They were subject to the authority of their fathers, viewed as little more than property. Membership within the community of the faithful will involve giving status to those who have none ... Hospitality, a major aspect of life in the ancient world, is to be extended to the most unlikely, thus challenging traditional notions of status. Hospitality to the unimportant will be a hallmark of the circle of Jesus' followers, as it was in Jesus' own ministry. And this has everything to do with faithfulness to the one whose rejection and death mark the way to glory.[1]*

Homiletical Directions

It is most often the case that when we see a Markan story in light of Mark's greater story, when we practice *narrative analogy*, we open up all kinds of possibilities for preaching. A sermon on faith and unbelief could easily arise out of our reading. In today's text the disciples continue to be *afraid*; they fail to *understand.* That raises before us the many texts in Mark which talk about *faith* or *fear* as the basic response to Jesus. The nuanced story in Mark 9:14-29 opens up another way of talking about our human response to Jesus. It might be that we are like the father of the boy with the unclean spirit. We believe and disbelieve at the same time! This is probably true of most of those to whom you preach. A sermon centering in these stories can work both to challenge people in their *unbelieving* and comfort people in their *believing.*

The closing verses of today's text about welcoming the children into the kingdom of God are also a fruitful path for preaching.

It would seem, however, that the response of the disciples might be the most important line to pursue. Story One could go back to the Parable of the Sower and remind people of the nature of the rocky ground. The disciples appear to be linked to this rocky ground metaphor. Story Two might be just a reminder of the three boat scenes and the three responses to Jesus' "passion/resurrection" predictions. These are rocky ground people indeed!

Story Three in this sermon option would deal with the betrayal and flight and denial on the part of the disciples in Mark 14. This gives us a wonderful opportunity to make use of the Mark 14 material. This should be the most extensive part of your storytelling this week. The story might focus on Judas and *betrayal*, the disciples and their *flight* ("You will all *fall away,*" Mark 14:27; 4:17) and Peter and his *denial.* (His *threefold* denial!)

The gospel word for this sermon begins with the *Nevertheless*! Nevertheless, the risen Jesus sends word to his disciples to meet him in Galilee as he had told them (Mark 16:6-7). After the betrayal, flight, and denial — before the day of resurrection — Jesus died on the cross as he had predicted. Somehow this means that betrayal, flight, and denial can be forgiven by Jesus. As the bearer of resurrection life he can wash away the deeds of the disciples and call them to Galilee to begin a new day of ministry.

Through this story Jesus seems to be saying something like this to us today. "I see you when you betray me. Your betrayal sent me to the cross. I have risen from the grave to call you to new life in me beyond the times of betrayal.

145

"I see you when you run away, fall away, from me. Your flight went with me to the cross. I have risen from the grave to call you to new life in me beyond the times of falling away.

"I see you in your times of denial. Your denial went with me to the cross. I have risen from the grave to call you to new life in me beyond the times of denial."

That's enough. The sermon can end there. If you want to put a stronger accent on the cross you can continue with Jesus saying: "Your sins nailed me to the cross. God has raised me from the cross to new life. I call upon you to follow me to new life. Follow me to Galilee. Rise, take up your cross, and follow. Amen."

---

1. Donald H. Juel, *Mark* (Minneapolis: Augsburg, 1990), pp. 133-134.

Mark 9:38-50

Mary Ann Tolbert sets this week's text in its larger context:

> *In good rhetorical fashion, the last two Passion prediction*
> *units (9:30—10:31 and 10:32-52) reiterate and expand*
> *this depiction of the disciples by constantly contrasting*
> *their actions and words with Jesus' teachings.[1]*

We observe that following Jesus' second "passion/resurrection" prediction it is noted that the disciples did not *understand*; they were *afraid* to ask (Mark 9:32). In the next verses the disciples are thinking about glory even while Jesus seeks to teach them about the cross. Their concern is only with themselves. "Who among us is the greatest?" is the best they can do after hearing Jesus' second "passion/resurrection" prediction (Mark 9:33-34). Today's text picks up at this point. The disciples have heard Jesus say that the greatest in the reign of God must be last of all and servant of all. Immediately they do the opposite. They proceed to prohibit one of these servants of God's reign from casting out demons.

In Mark 10:13-16 we see the disciples countermanding the words of Jesus once again. Jesus has explicitly told the disciples that to receive a child is to receive Jesus. They proceed, however, to rebuke those who wish to bring children to Jesus (10:13).

Tolbert again:

> *The central part of the second Passion prediction unit is*
> *composed of an **inclusio** about receiving children (9:36-*
> *37 and 10:13-16), surrounding three episodes that focus*
> *in different ways on the proper treatment of weak or*
> *disenfranchised people: the alien exorciser (9:38-41), the*
> *"little ones" (9:42-50), and the divorced wife (10:2-12).*

*The element of the **inclusio** itself dramatizes the disciples'*
continuing waywardness.[2]

There is another possible way of setting today's text in its broader narrative context. The man casting out demons (10:38) is clearly an *outsider*. The first word we heard in Mark's Gospel about outsiders is in the Parable of the Sower. In explaining his parable to his disciples Jesus said: "To you has been given the secret of the kingdom of God; but for those *outside*, everything comes in parables ..." (Mark 4:11). It appears at first glance that the disciples are the true *insiders*. The third boat scene, however, seems to turn these insiders into outsiders, as we have observed earlier. In explaining the reality of outsiders, Jesus says that they are those who can look but not perceive, listen but not understand (Mark 4:12). In the third boat scene (Mark 8:13-21) Jesus says that it is the disciples who have hardened (rocky ground) hearts. It is the disciples who have eyes but fail to see, ears and fail to hear. Jesus appears to turn the whole notion of insider and outsider inside out and backwards with these words to the disciples.

In today's text Jesus issues a stern warning on how to care for outsiders who are deemed to be "little ones" (Mark 9:42ff.). Most commentators say that the "little ones" are not necessarily children although children would not be excluded. We referred earlier to the characteristics of the "little ones" in Mark's Gospel. David Rhoads and Donald Michie point out that Mark consistently introduces "little people" in his narrative: "They are 'flat' characters with several consistent traits which they share in common: a childlike, often persistent, faith; a disregard for personal status and power; and a capacity for sacrificial service. In the words of Jesus, they are the 'little ones who have faith.' "[3] Quite often in Mark's Gospel it is precisely the "little ones" who bear fruit thirty, sixty and a hundredfold!

Homiletical Directions

The theme of insiders and outsiders might be the best center for a sermon on today's text. The text is full of surprises about who the outsiders are and who the insiders are. Earlier we referred to a professor of theology who once said: "Whenever you want to draw lines in order to mark who is outside the kingdom and who is inside, always remember: *Jesus is on the other side of the line! Jesus is always with the outsiders!*" That thought stands behind our story telling for today.

The context set by Tolbert's comments form a good context for our sermon. She has pointed out that in the section headed by the second "passion/resurrection" prediction (Mark 9:30—10:31) there are stories about receiving children (9:33-37 and 10:13-16) which surround stories about an alien exorciser, the "little ones," and a divorced woman. In her words, the weak and the disenfranchised are welcomed to the kingdom! Our first story telling task, therefore, would be to highlight this context for our listeners. It is of particular importance that the stories which boundary today's text about receiving children be told in some fullness. Jesus is on the side of the children! "To receive such a child is to receive me," Jesus says.

Our second story task would be to tell the story of the alien exorciser. The disciples see him as an outsider. Jesus does not! The story is very brief in the Markan text, but we can expand it quite easily by imagining the disciples eavesdropping on this man, watching what he does, detailing their plans for presenting their case to Jesus. The disciples are diligent! They want to be sure that outsiders remain as outsiders. In fact, the disciples seem to be the experts in naming outsiders. They also rebuke those who would bring children to Jesus (10:13) when Jesus has already told them that to receive such a child is to receive him.

Story Three could examine the inside/outside status of the disciples. The context set by Tolbert centers in the failure of the disciples. We also related this story to the insider/outsider language of the Parable of the Sower. Jesus tells the disciples that they are the insiders (Mark 4:11). Later, however, he reprimands the disciples by telling them that they possess the precise characteristics of outsiders (Mark 4:11-12; 8:16-21). The story of the disciples told in Mark is a hard-hitting story against all self-righteousness. When insiders start deciding who the outsiders are, as the disciples do, they walk in real danger. Such a story cuts hard against any contemporary persons who see themselves as insiders and make all kinds of conclusions based on their self-proclaimed "insider" status. These stories are hard stories for any who wish to make distinctions between outsiders and insiders.

The good news of the closing proclamation is the news that Jesus is on the side of the outsiders. Those in our congregations who worry about their status in God's eyes or those who have been labeled as outsiders will hear these stories and this proclamation with glad hearts. "I am on the side of outsiders!" Jesus says to us through these stories. "I am on the side of the weak. I am on the side of the 'little ones.' I am on the side of children and those with childlike faith."

> *Let the little children come to me; do not stop them; for it is to such as these that the kingdom of God belongs.*
> (Mark 10:14).

1. Mary Ann Tolbert, *Sowing the Gospel* (Minneapolis: Fortress Press, 1989), p. 209.

2. *Ibid.*, p. 210.

3. David Rhoads and Donald Michie, *Mark As Story* (Philadelphia: Fortress Press, 1982), p. 130.

Mark 10:2-16

We have understood this entire section of Mark's Gospel from 8:22—10:52 as a journey "on the way" to Jerusalem. The clues to the movement of this "way" are not many. Mark 10:1 does indicate that Jesus is closing in on the Holy City. It was standard practice in oral cultures to tell a "journey story" as a way of incorporating a variety of matters that may be only loosely related to each other.

In the previous chapter we made reference to Mary Ann Tolbert's contention that this central section of the "passion/resurrection" predictions and the journey "on the way" to Jerusalem deals with the proper treatment of the weak and disenfranchised. She speaks of the alien exorciser (9:38-41), the "little ones" (9:42-50) and the divorced wife from today's passage as examples of Jesus' care for the weak. Tolbert's comments help to set this passage into its wider narrative context.

Women certainly needed protection in Jesus' day. "... in Jewish law a woman was regarded as a thing. She had no legal rights whatever but was at the complete disposal of the male head of the family. The result was that a man could divorce his wife on almost any grounds."[1] The Old Testament passage on which easy divorce was grounded is Deuteronomy 24:1:

> *Suppose a man enters into marriage with a woman, but she does not please him because he finds something **objectionable** about her, and so he writes a certificate of divorce, puts it in her hand, and sends her out of his house ... .*

Through the centuries the debate among Jewish teachers centered on what *objectionable* or *indecent* things could serve as a cause for giving a divorce certificate. One school taught that adultery alone was the indecent thing for which a man could put a

woman away. (Only women could commit adultery in this system!)
Another school of thought deemed all kinds of behavior as
justifiable grounds for sending a wife packing. "Human nature
being as it is, it was the laxer view which prevailed. The result was
that divorce for the most trivial reasons ... was tragically common."[2]

Jesus must be seen here to be speaking on behalf of the rights
of women. He totally disregards rabbinic teaching on this matter
and, as a teacher himself (!), he follows the analogy of Scripture.
Scripture is the best interpreter of Scripture. So Jesus reminds his
hearers of another biblical story. (Jesus *thinks in stories*!) The
commandment of Moses (Deuteronomy 24) was only given because
of the hardness of human hearts, Jesus says. But that's not the way
things are supposed to be. That was not the Creator's intention in
the beginning. The intention from the beginning was that two
become one flesh. "Therefore what God has joined together, let no
one separate." Jesus here strikes a blow at a longstanding tradition
which treated women with contempt. He stands as a champion of
the weak and the little ones. Such is ever the good news of the
Gospel!

What is not stated but perhaps implied in Jesus' dialogue is
that human hardness of heart (rocky ground) is not the ultimate
destiny of the human race. Jesus has come to give a *new heart* to
sinful humans.

> But this is the covenant that I will make with the house of
> Israel after those days, says the Lord: I will write it on
> their hearts; and I will be their God, and they shall be my
> people.
>
> (Jeremiah 31:33)

In his institution of the Lord's Supper Jesus says over the cup:
"This is my blood of the *covenant,* which is poured out for many"
(Mark 14:24). One way of thinking about the Lord's Supper is that
it is a meal through which Jesus works to "write upon our hearts,"
to make our hearts new, to make new persons out of us—persons
who bear fruit thirtyfold, sixtyfold and a hundredfold. For such
persons might there not be a world of changed human hearts where

a law of divorce, given because of hardened human hearts, is no longer necessary?

Jesus comes bringing the kingdom of God near (Mark 1:15). "The nearness of the kingdom of God implies new possibilities; it means acknowledging God's will that a union between a man and a woman should be permanent and that divorce laws must be understood accordingly." [3] It also means that beyond the shattering experience of divorce, people's hearts can still be reached with the love that transforms. Such people are most certainly free to start over again in terms of marriage.

Homiletical Direction

Divorce is a crucial matter in our society today. We all know the statistics and the result of those statistics in people's lives. People long to hear a word from the Church on this issue. Today's text provides us with a rare opportunity to address this tragic area of human life. We will probably address this matter best by setting forth the clear *teaching* of this text and the Bible on divorce. For this reason a narrative, story telling approach to today's text is not recommended. *Teaching* is recommended!

In teaching on this text there are several main points that need to be addressed:

1. Divorce is a violation of the will of the Creator. It doesn't matter that divorce is quite acceptable in our society. It is not acceptable to God. People who have divorced are sinners in need of repentance. There is no short cut around this need of repentance. We are a people called to repent on account of our sinfulness. Divorce is not the sin of sins which calls for special repentance. Divorce is sin, a breaking down of human relationships, which calls for repentance as do all of our sinful behaviors. Divorce is one of the tragic behaviors that arise out of the hardness of the human heart. Divorce is failure in the eyes of God and in the eyes of those whose lives are shattered through this experience. Divorce calls us to repentance.

2. There is forgiveness for repentant, divorced persons just as there is forgiveness for repentant sinners in other areas of human behavior that violate God's will. The Jewish culture accommodated

itself to divorce. Men could put away their wives for any reason at all. They justified their behavior on the basis of the law of Moses in Deuteronomy. Jesus challenged this justification for divorce. The law of Moses was given only because of people's hardened hearts. Jesus Christ has come as the Sower of the Word so that good seed might fall upon hardened hearts and transform them into good soil for the gospel. Jesus' word of forgiveness does not just wipe away past sins. Jesus' word of forgiveness is a life-transforming word. It is a word with the power to change us. It is a word that can convert hearts of stone. It is a word that gives us new life.

If this point is made in the sermon we could quite properly lead people through an action of repentance and forgiveness in the midst of our sermon. Ask the people to bow their heads and ask forgiveness for all their sins and particularly for the ways they have violated human relationships. After silence for a moment of quiet repentance we can announce the good news. Jesus' word for you today is, "I am the One who bathes hardened hearts with the water of my grace. Your sins are forgiven. I give you a new heart. I give you a new heart that you might enter human relationships in the future out of the power of my transforming love. Something new awaits you!"

3. Transformed persons can do new things. The closing words in today's text appear to forbid remarriage. To marry another is to commit adultery. The gospel insight here is that hard-hearted persons will continue to make the same mistakes. It is best not to remarry at all! But persons transformed by the grace of God can do new things! They can marry again in the hope that a new relationship on the other side of hard hearts, repentance and forgiveness is possible!

4. The congregation is to receive "divorced sinners" with an attitude of love. Divorced persons often feel cut off from their former communities. They tell us that they do not feel welcome in our churches. Let this not be so in the community of God's "transformed" people! Jesus Christ came to call sinners to repentance. Our congregations must not cut asunder what God wills to bind together with us. In words and deeds our doors must

always be open to "divorced sinners." In words and deeds our doors must always be open to all sinners!

---

1. William Barclay, *The Gospel of Mark* (Philadelphia: Westminster Press, 1975), p. 238.

2. *Ibid.*, p. 239.

3. Donald H. Juel, *Mark* (Minneapolis: Augsburg, 1990), p. 138.

Mark 10:17-31

Today's text begins with the story of the man who ran to Jesus in order to ask him what he must *do* to inherit eternal life. This request for something to *do* follows immediately upon Jesus' word that the kingdom of God welcomes children. In other words, we have just heard from the lips of Jesus that the kingdom of God is to be *received as a gift*, received as children receive. Then comes a man who wishes to *achieve the kingdom as a reward*. The fundamental meaning of the gospel is at stake in these two postures. The gospel of the kingdom comes as a gift we receive! That's the point. The man who ran and knelt at Jesus' feet did not understand this. He wanted to *do*! He wanted to *achieve*! We should expect immediately that he will go away sorrowful.

In chapter 17 we examined this story in light of two similar stories in Mark's Gospel which serve as examples of the *thorny ground* in the Parable of the Sower. "And others are those sown among the thorns; these are the ones who hear the word, but the cares of the world, and the *lure of wealth*, and the desire for other things come in and choke the word, and it yields nothing" (Mark 4:18-19). For this man it was the "lure of wealth" that choked out the possibility of the kingdom come near. (Please refer to chapter 17 where this man is placed in the company of King Herod and Pilate. If you did not do so earlier, here is a chance to stitch these three stories together for this week's sermon.)

This section of Mark's Gospel has much in the way of teaching for the life of the early Christian community. Donald H. Juel points out that a community that has a sustained existence must come to terms with the proper place and proper use of possessions. The man in this story, a man of great possessions, is sent away. He yields no fruit. Jesus hammers home the message. "How hard it will be for those who have wealth to enter the kingdom of God! ...

It is easier for a camel to go through the eye of a needle than for someone who is rich to enter the kingdom of God" (Mark 10:23, 25). The early chapters of the book of Acts also deal with possessions as an important facet of community life (Acts 2:42-47; 3:1-10; 5:1-11).

It is clear that early Christians struggled with matters of poverty and wealth. It is usually assumed that the early Christians were drawn primarily from the bottom strata of the economic scale. Though this may be true, it is also clear that they viewed wealth as a sign of God's blessing. The disciples appear to hold this view. Thus they are incredulous when Jesus turns the rich man away. The disciples may have understood the rich man to be among the first and most important people in town. Jesus sees it differently: "... many who are first will be last, and the last will be first" (Mark 10:31). Jesus turns cultural expectations upside down.

On this matter of "last-being-first" we might remember what we said earlier about those Jesus welcomes in the stories that immediately precede this one. Jesus welcomes children and the "little ones." He welcomes an alien exorciser to his fold. He stands with women with no rights in divorce proceedings. With Jesus, indeed, the last are first! Jesus also turns religious expectations upside down.

The disciples were impressed with the rich man who ran and knelt at Jesus' feet. When Jesus turned him away they were incredulous. "Then who can be saved?" they blurt out to Jesus. It is clear to them that this rich man is a very good man, a man blessed by God. He had kept all the commandments. He had *done* it all! If he can't be saved, who can be? Good questions. Wonderful questions. Questions that lead us again to the fundamental center of the gospel message. Who can be saved? "For mortals it is impossible, but not for God; for God all things are possible" (Mark 10:27). For God in Jesus Christ it is possible to welcome children to the kingdom. For Jesus it is possible to welcome the "little ones." For Jesus it is possible to welcome the alien exorciser (Mark 9:38-39). For Jesus it is possible to welcome women who have been put out of their houses. For Jesus it is possible to welcome the last and name them "First." This is precisely what the gospel of Jesus Christ is about. God in Jesus Christ saves sinners. "Those who are well have no need of a physician, but those who are sick; I have come to call not the righteous but sinners" (Mark 2:17).

Homiletical Directions

We have already mentioned the possibility with this text of combining it with the stories of King Herod and Pilate as examples of "thorny ground." Stitching these stories together has the effect of a challenge to discipleship!

We said above that in this text Jesus turns cultural and religious expectations upside down. Let's start first with the turning around of *cultural* expectations. The cultural expectation was that if you were rich you were blessed by God. That's just the way the world works. We can hear this exact message from our culture any day of the week. Our culture rewards the "lifestyle of the rich and famous" with special television programming and favor. Even Christian preachers sometimes boast of riches as a sign of God's glory in our lives!

Story One here would be the textual story, putting strong emphasis on Jesus' words about the difficulty of riches. The contrast at the end of the story is stark: "… many who are first will be last, and the last will be first." Let these images live in people's minds. Here is a story that counters the expectations of our culture. Every one of our listeners knows that. In telling this story we may perhaps enlarge the imagination of those who hear. There might be a different way of looking at status in a society.

Story Two would move to one or more of the stories in Acts where we find the early church struggling with this matter of wealth. (See above for reference to these passages.) If you want to tell a real shocker, tell the story of Ananias and Sapphira in Acts 5!

The goal of telling these stories would be simple. These are stories that challenge our culture's stories about wealth and poverty. We tell such stories to transform the imagination of our hearers. Obedience to the gospel grows partially out of a new imagination!

Close the sermon with the line from Jesus about the last being first. Ours is a culture that celebrates *firstness*! Every athletic team and business and person in our culture wants to be No. 1!

158

Being No. 1 comes close to being the highest value in our culture. We either want to be No. 1 or at least be associated with someone or something that is No. 1. Into such a world Jesus' word falls hard. "... many who are first will be last, and the last will be first."

Another sermon possibility on this text would deal with the way Jesus upsets *religious* expectations. Story One might be the story of the text told in all the richness of detail and imagination that you can pack into it. The focus in the telling should be on the rich man who wants to *do* for the kingdom. He wants to *achieve* eternal life. He goes away sorrowful.

Who then can be saved? This question leads to other stories. Some of the stories from this section of Mark's Gospel (9:30— 10:52) can be told in answer to the question: Who can be saved? Many of the stories are about *receiving* the kingdom as a *gift*. Who is greatest in the kingdom? A child (9:33-37). Who is included in the kingdom? An alien exorciser (9:38-41). Whom does God wish to protect? The "little ones" (9:42) and the divorced ones (10:2-9). Who can be saved? "Let the little children come to me; do not stop them; for it is to such as these that the kingdom of God belongs" (10:14).

Having told these stories we are ready for our closing proclamation. The question is ripe for our time. Who can be saved? If this wonderful man in the text can't be saved, who can be? We don't measure up to him at all. How about us? How about sinners? Jesus says: "I have come to call not the righteous, but sinners. I have come to welcome children and all who receive me as a child receives. I have come to welcome the weak and the outcast. I have come to make the last, first. Who can be saved? You can be saved! Sound impossible? I have come to make all things possible. I have come to make your salvation possible. Amen."

Mark 10:35-45

The first thing to note about the appointment of today's text from Mark's Gospel is that which is omitted. Last week's text ended at Mark 10:31. This week's text begins with Mark 10:35. Mark 10:32-34 is omitted from the lectionary. These omitted verses are among the most important verses in Mark's Gospel. They compose the *third* "passion/resurrection" prediction of Jesus. (See Mark 8:31; 9:30-31.) These texts were treated as a whole in chapter 21. It would be well if you would re-read that chapter in preparation for this week's sermon work. Jesus' "passion/resurrection" predictions and the "glory" response of the disciples are at the very center of Mark's theology of the cross! If you haven't treated this material as a *whole* before, this would be a good occasion to do so.

Mark consistently portrays Jesus "on the way" to the cross. The disciples who travel "on the way" with Jesus never seem to understand the matter of the cross. These rocky-ground disciples are deaf and blind to the words and actions of Jesus (8:17-21). Every time Jesus points them to the cross they talk about glory. This is true in this week's appointed verses from Mark. The response of the disciples to Jesus' third "passion/resurrection" prediction is a clamor for *glory*. James and John ask Jesus: "Grant us to sit, one at your right hand and one at your left, in your glory" (Mark 10:37).

Jesus, in reply, asks the disciples if they are able to drink the cup that he will drink. (On the image of the cup see: Isaiah 51:17, 22; Lamentations 4:21.) He asks them if they are able to endure baptism with him. "We are able," they say. Jesus acknowledges that they, too, will endure the cup and the baptism; "... but to sit at my right hand or at my left is not mine to grant, but it is for those for whom it has been prepared" (Mark 10:40). Those for whom it has been prepared are two criminals. Criminals are the ones at the right and left hand of Jesus in the glory of the cross (Mark 15:27).

Jesus then proceeds to teach his disciples the true nature of his ministry, the true nature of servant leadership in his community. "… whoever wishes to be great among you must be your servant, and whoever wishes to be first among you must be slave of all." This is not what Jesus' disciples had in mind when they asked about sharing in his glory! The disciples think glory. Jesus thinks cross. This is an absolute base conviction of Mark's Gospel. We are at the heart of the matter here! Jesus has come to die. Jesus has come to make a journey "on the way" to Jerusalem and Golgotha. "… the Son of Man will be handed over to the chief priests and the scribes, and they will condemn him to death; then they will hand him over to the Gentiles; they will mock him, and spit upon him, and flog him, and kill him; and after three days he will rise again" (Mark 8:33-34).

On the other side of the cross there is the hope of resurrection. The resurrection will validate Jesus' way to the cross as God's way in the world. God's way in the world is the way of giving one's life. "For the Son of Man came not to be served but to serve, and to give his life a ransom for many" (Mark 10:45). The Greek word for *ransom* denotes the price paid for the redemption of a slave. It is a word that has figured strongly in the church's attempt to understand the ministry of Jesus. We are familiar with the "ransom" theory of the atonement. Jesus had to pay with his life to redeem us from the manifold forms of slavery that bind us.

Mark 10:45 is Mark's only use of the word *ransom*. Matthew 20:28 is the only other use of this word in our Gospels. Saint Paul does not use the word at all, though he does refer to the "price" that had to be paid for us and to Jesus' work of *redemption* (Romans 3:24-25; 1 Corinthians 6:20; Galatians 1:4, 3:14). Commentators often look to Isaiah 53 as the Old Testament background for the work of Jesus' ministry that is presented to us in today's verses. Some believe that these verses from Mark are a kind of summary of his understanding of Jesus. It is not surprising that such a summary comes on the brink of Jesus' entrance into Jerusalem!

Homiletical Directions

It is absolutely imperative that our sermon work for this week center in Mark's theology of the cross. This week's verses explicate this theology very well. This "cross theology" was difficult for Jesus to explicate to his disciples; it was difficult for Mark to explicate to us; and it is difficult for us to explicate it for our hearers today. So many modern-day hearers of the gospel are just like the disciples. No matter how much we may talk of cross — they think glory! There are many Christian teachers among us today who have simply sold out to "glory theology." They present the Christian life as a glory road! If you truly believe in Jesus your life will be wonderful. If you truly believe in Jesus you will live beyond want. If you truly believe in Jesus you will live a glory-filled life in all of its aspects.

How different this is from the message of the Gospel of Mark! Mark paints the picture of a Savior "on the way" to Jerusalem, on the way to the cross. Mark paints the picture of true disciples as those who "... deny themselves and take up their cross and follow me. For those who want to save their life will lose it, and those who lose their life for my sake, and for the sake of the gospel, will save it" (Mark 8:34-35).

We have suggested above that one possibility of preaching this text would be to set it in context with the other "passion/resurrection" texts. Chapter 21 treats these texts in their overarching unity.

Our sermon work could also focus on the words about *ransom*. One or two stories would lead us to the key text (10:45). Story One would be a brief summary of the flow of the three "passion/resurrection" predictions and the disciples' continued response of glory. Today's text needs this whole contextual background even if it is just briefly told.

Story Two could highlight the great vision of Isaiah (52:13—53:12). Israel's hopes were shaped by the expectation of a Suffering Servant who "... was despised and rejected by others; a man of suffering and acquainted with infirmity; and as one from whom others hide their faces he was despised, and we held him of no account" (Isaiah 53:3). This is the One who was prophesied. This is the One who will give his life as a ransom for us. "Surely he has borne our infirmities and carried our diseases; yet we accounted him stricken, struck down by God, and afflicted. But he was wounded for our transgressions, crushed for our iniquities; upon him was the punishment that made us whole..." (Isaiah 53:4-5).

Story Three would be the story of the text leading to the Son of Man who gives his life as ransom. The best way to treat Jesus as the "ransom for many" is to do so through proclamation. Try to avoid *theories of atonement*. This is not class time. This is sermon time. This is proclamation time.

A word of proclamation to come at the end of these stories would be something like this: "Through these stories Jesus speaks to us this day. He says, 'I have come to fulfill Isaiah's dream. I have come to bear your infirmities. I have come to be wounded for your transgressions. I have come to bless your life with the blessing of God. You may not want my blessing. You may wish to condemn me. You may wish to kill me. Very well. Have your way. Push me out of the world and onto a cross. I will go through the cross to bless you. I will go through hell itself to bless you. I have come to give my life as a ransom for many.' Amen."

Another way to come to the ransom aspect of today's text would be to retell many Markan stories that demonstrate the *captivity* of people who come to Jesus. Mark 1:21-28 tells the story of a man in captivity to demonic powers. Mark 1:40-45 tells the story of a man in captivity to the dread disease of leprosy. Mark 2:1-12 tells the story of a man captive to sin and paralysis. Mark 5:25-34 tells the story of a woman captive to a twelve-year flow of blood. There are many other stories as well.

You might prefer to tell stories of modern people in their multiple captivities rather than biblical stories. In either case the proclamation which closes this sermon would go something like this: "I am the Son of Man who has come to serve you. I have come to give my life as a ransom. I have come to redeem you from all your captivities. I have come to ransom your life from sin. I have come to ransom your life from the powers of evil. I have come to ransom your life from death. I have come to suffer and die that you might live and serve under the sign of the cross. Amen."

163

Mark 10:46-52

We come now to the end of Part One of Mark's Gospel. Part One goes from chapters 1-10 of Mark. This section of the Gospel centers on Jesus, Sower of the Word, alive in ministry and "on the way" to Jerusalem. Part Two of Mark's Gospel is chapters 11-16. These chapters take place in Jerusalem. The plot synopsis of these chapters is the Parable of the Tenants in Mark 12:1-11. This is the story of the "beloved son" sent by the owner of the vineyard and killed by the wicked tenants.

The last section of Part One is Mark 8:22—10:52. The prelude to this section is the ongoing blindness and deafness of the disciples. "Do you have eyes, and fail to see?" Jesus asks his disciples (Mark 8:18). The disciples have been insiders to Jesus' ministry from the beginning, but they still fail to see. They are blind.

The blindness of the disciples sets the stage for the last section of Part One of Mark's story. The disciples — the insiders — do not see. Human eyes, it appears, cannot see the meaning and destiny of the figure of Jesus in their midst. God will have to open blind eyes to enable humans to see what is there to be seen. This section of Mark's Gospel, therefore, begins and ends with the story of the healing of a blind man. Jesus opened the eyes of a blind man in Bethsaida (Mark 8:22-26). This section of the Gospel closes with today's text of the healing of a blind man in Jericho. In between these stories lie Jesus' three "passion/resurrection" predictions, which the disciples did not understand at all. Jesus talks about cross and they insistently think of glory, their glory! Their eyes are not open to see.

The message of the structure of this section is that only God can open our eyes to grasp the nature and destiny of Jesus Christ. This week's text is about such "eye opening" work. It takes place in Jericho, just down the road from Jesus' destination: Jerusalem.

As Jesus was leaving Jericho with his disciples a great multitude was with him. A blind man by the name of Bartimaeus was sitting by the roadside as the triumphal procession to Jerusalem passed him by. When the blind man heard that it was Jesus who was passing him by "...he began to shout out and say, 'Jesus, Son of David, have mercy on me!' No one could stop him from shouting out. Finally, Jesus heard the shouts and attended the needs of the blind man. Bartimaeus ran to Jesus. 'What do you want me to do for you?' Jesus asked. 'My teacher, let me see again,' he said. And Jesus said to him, 'Go; your faith has made you well.' Immediately he regained his sight and *followed him on the way.*"

A word needs to be said here about the cry of Bartimaeus to Jesus, naming him as "Son of David." Jack Dean Kingsbury puts the matter well:

> *Because Jesus has not heretofore appeared in Mark's story as the Son of David, this pericope plays a pivotal role in conveying to the reader Mark's sense of this title. To begin with, Mark affirms with it that Jesus is indeed of the lineage of David. Unlike Matthew and Luke, Mark has no genealogy that links Jesus with the line of David ... it appears that it is exactly the Davidic descent of Jesus which is being attested to when Bartimaeus addresses "Jesus of Nazareth" as "Son of David ... ."*[1]

Part Two of Mark's Gospel which begins in Mark 11:1 will emphasize this "Son of David" theme. The entry into Jerusalem, for example, is loaded with messianic images. The confession of Bartimaeus, therefore, prepares us for a shift in emphasis in Mark's storytelling as we move into Part Two of the Gospel.

Some commentators believe that in this climactic story of Part One of his Gospel Mark portrays Bartimaeus as a kind of model of the Christian life. The Bartimaeus story is truly a story of what happens when God in Jesus Christ opens blind eyes. Here is what happens when Jesus' word falls on *good soil*! If that is so, we see that the Christian life begins with persistent pleading. "Jesus, have mercy on me!" That is the prayer of good-soil people. We come to Jesus in our need and in confession. Jesus does not turn Bartimaeus,

Jesus does not turn sinners, Jesus does not turn us away when we come to him pleading for mercy. "Go," Jesus says, "your faith has made you well." "Go and your eyes will be opened. Go and you will see me truly." And so we follow Jesus *on the way*. Bartimaeus, by the way, is the first person in Mark's telling of the story who follows Jesus after Jesus acts on his behalf. With eyes wide open we, too, are ready to follow Jesus to Jerusalem. With eyes wide open we are ready to take up the cross and follow the Crucified One.

Homiletical Directions

If we choose to treat this text in its narrative connections we will treat it as the end of this very important section of Mark's Gospel (8:22—10:52). The matter before us is that of human blindness in the light of Jesus' self-revelation. Story One will set up this section of Mark's Gospel by rehearsing the difficulties of sight in the lives of the disciples as they move through the opening chapters, climaxing in 8:17-22.

Story Two can set the context of today's story in Mark 8:22—10:52. This is a section that is boundaried by stories of the healing of the blind. In the middle of these stories we have Jesus' "passion/resurrection" predictions to which the disciples constantly reply with hopes of glory. They still fail to see!

Story Three: enter Bartimaeus. He sees! Jesus opens his eyes. He is a man of faith. Faith is clearly defined in this story as "coming to Jesus for mercy!" Therein lies our hope for opened eyes. If the disciples didn't grasp the nature of the Sower, then what is to assure us that we will do any better than the disciples? Our best posture is the posture of faith that pleads and receives. Good soil is *receptive* soil! Let the seed fall on us, Jesus. Open our eyes. With eyes opened we will follow you on the way!

A sermon with these three stories might well end in prayer. The prayer we pray should put us in the shoes of Bartimaeus. We come to our prayer, that is, blind and pleading. We pray that we might be receptive soil. We pray that Jesus may open our eyes. We pray for the strength to follow on the way of the cross. The assurance of our prayer is that Jesus came to open blind eyes. Jesus opened the eyes of Bartimaeus. Jesus will open our eyes as well. Go! Your faith has made you well!

---

1. Jack Dean Kingsbury, *The Christology of Mark's Gospel* (Philadelphia: Fortress Press, 1983), p. 106.

Mark 11:1-11

"When they were approaching Jerusalem ...." These words open the Palm Sunday text. Jerusalem has been the destination of Jesus for the last several chapters in Mark. We come, therefore, to a geographical shift in the location of the action in the Gospel of Mark. We move from Galilee to Jerusalem. We also move from Part One to Part Two of Mark's Gospel.

Mary Ann Tolbert has given detailed attention to this shift in the story. She notes that each part of Mark's Gospel begins with a kind of summary of the action that will follow. Mark 1:14-15 announces that Jesus came into Galilee, where Part One of the story will take place. He came preaching the Gospel. He came as the Sower of the Word! The words of Jesus give full expression to what is to come: "The time is fulfilled, and the kingdom of God has come near; repent, and believe in the good news" (Mark 1:15). Part One of Mark's story is set in Galilee, Jesus sows the Word, people are called to believe the Word they have heard. The plot synopsis of Part One, the Parable of the Sower (Mark 4:1-20), makes it clear that there will be a variety of ways in which people hear the Word. We have spoken much about the Parable of the Sower as the plot synopsis of Part One of Mark's Gospel.

Mark 11:1 announces the geographical change. Jesus leaves Galilee. He comes to Jerusalem. The role of Jesus in this part of the Gospel is proclaimed by the crowd. "Hosanna! ... Blessed is the coming kingdom of our ancestor David" (Mark 11:9-10). In Part One of the Gospel the emphasis was on the *message*. In Part Two, the emphasis is on the *nature of the messenger.* "Both of these elements, however, are part of the *same* interconnected and interwoven story, for the preacher of God's good news is the heir of David's throne in a world deeply gone awry."[1] The plot synopsis for this part of Mark's story is the Parable of the Tenants in the

Vineyard (Mark 12:1-11). The "heir of the vineyard," the "beloved son," is killed by wicked and evil men.

Tolbert points out, furthermore, that Mark 1:1-11 also introduces some of the "major shifts of emphasis that characterize the second part." For the first time in the Gospel story Jesus knows in advance what is to happen in the immediate future. He sends his disciples ahead into a village to secure a colt for his entry into Jerusalem. Nearly every word in the story rings out with overtones of Old Testament imagery. Another striking difference between this story and what has gone before is the *public* acclamation of Jesus' identity. All through Part One of Mark Jesus asks that his identity be kept secret. Now, however, the whole world is to know![2] "Then those who went ahead and those who followed were *shouting*, 'Hosanna! Blessed is the one who comes in the name of the Lord!' " (Mark 11:9).

The standard commentaries and the footnotes in a good Bible give us the many Old Testament references in these few verses. Mark has not drawn so heavily on the Hebrew Bible before in telling his story. There is an obvious signal here that the event taking place, the entry into Jerusalem, is of utmost importance to our storyteller!

One of the Old Testament stories that is seldom given as a reference but which is of great importance in grasping the nature of this event is 1 Kings 1. This story comes at the end of one of the two oldest pieces of Hebrew literature, the Succession Document: 2 Samuel 6:16 — 1 Kings 2:46. This document is understood by many students of the Bible as the story of the succession of Solomon to David's throne. How was it that Solomon succeeded David? That was one of the most important questions that the people of Israel ever asked. The Succession Document gives the answer.

The theme of the Succession Document is stated clearly in 1 Kings 1:20, 27: "... who should sit on the throne of my lord the king after him?" David answered the question by saying that God had revealed to him that it would be Solomon (vv. 29-30). David then called for Zadok the priest, Nathan the prophet, and Benaiah the son of Jehoida and told them to make preparations for a royal coronation. Solomon was to ride to the coronation on a mule! (v.

169

33). The trumpet was to blow, and when it blew the people shouted: "Long live King Solomon" (vv. 34, 39). "And all the people went up following him, playing on pipes and rejoicing with great joy, so that the earth quaked at their noise" (v. 40).

This story of Solomon's coronation is clearly the model for what happened on Palm Sunday. Jesus took action to make the entry into Jerusalem an event parallel with this story of Solomon! It was clear to everyone on hand that day what was happening. A king was ascending his throne. A coronation was in progress.

The people must have loved it! They had been waiting a thousand years for this event. "Are you the one who is to come or do we look for another?" That was the question of the ages in Israel. And now it had come to pass. The king was here. The promise was fulfilled. The time of power and glory and triumph was at hand. That is, of course, the irony of the whole event. The people who took part in this coronation entry into Jerusalem were filled to overflowing with hopes for this One. But we come to this event in the context of Mark's Gospel. We have heard Jesus utter three "passion/resurrection" predictions. We have heard it over and over that Jesus comes to Jerusalem to be delivered to the chief priests, to be condemned to death, to be spit upon and scourged and raised up on a tree of death. A king will be crowned. This is so. But the cross will be the place of coronation.

Homiletical Directions

Story One for a Palm Sunday sermon might begin in the Old Testament with the story we have referred to of Solomon's coronation in 1 Kings 1. This story, too, needs some background. The key messianic text in the Old Testament is 2 Samuel 7:8-16. This is God's promise to David that God would raise up David's offspring after him to rule in his place. "I will establish the throne of his kingdom forever," God says to David. "I will be a father to him, and he shall be a son to me ... Your house and your kingdom shall be made sure forever before me; your throne shall be established forever" (2 Samuel 7:13-14, 16). The coronation of Solomon is the first great fulfillment of this promise of an everlasting monarchy. God made a promise. The promise has been fulfilled.

That's the heart of the telling of these stories from 2 Samuel and 1 Kings.

The history of God's fulfillment of this promise, however, ran into hard times. The exile was the end of the monarchy! How was God to fulfill the promise now? For the most part Israel did not lose faith in God's promise. "Are you the one to come or are we to look for another?" Every generation of Israel raised this question. And then one day, there he was. Jesus rode into Jerusalem just like Solomon did! Telling the story of today's text with ample reference to Old Testament references can be our Second Story for today's sermon. It is a joyous story. God's word of promise is fulfilled. It's party time.

But ... those of us who come to this story through a reading of Mark's Gospel cannot be filled with joy. We have heard Jesus predict his passion three times: Mark 8:31; Mark 9:30-31; 10:32-34. We might want to tell of these "passion/resurrection" predictions in order to change our mood about this Palm Sunday joy! We know why Jesus enters Jerusalem. It is not to reign in triumph. It is to be hung on a cross.

The Palm Sunday story in itself is a story of great hope. We can celebrate. When we look *back*, however, we see these "passion/resurrection" predictions that darken the mood for us. When we look *forward* we encounter the same mood of darkness and foreboding. It might be well to tell at this point the story of the Parable of the Tenants. We have referred to this story as the plot synopsis of Part Two of Mark's Gospel. It is a story, however, that will not appear in the pericopes for the Markan year. Palm Sunday might be an appropriate time to tell this story which is so vital to Mark's carefully structured tale.

The Parable of the Tenants in the Vineyard is a story which casts instant light on the Palm Sunday story. The Heir of the Vineyard enters the city in triumph. This parable, however, makes it abundantly clear what it is that will happen to the Heir. "Finally he sent him (the beloved son!) to them, saying, 'They will respect my son.' But those tenants said to one another, 'This is the heir; come, let us kill him ... ' " (Mark 12:6-7).

Palm Sunday is, indeed, coronation Sunday! The God-promised king has come at last. This is the one we are looking for. But the world will have none of it. Evil raises its head. The "beloved son" is overpowered. He is condemned and murdered just as Jesus had foreseen. We learn something vitally important about God here. God does not come to overpower us. God does not come to override our human evil and impose a king upon us. God comes, rather, in the weakness of love. God is revealed in hiding, as Luther often said. God is revealed in a cross. God is revealed in death. This surely is a man of sorrows and acquainted with grief!

The word spoken to us by the "beloved son" who rides in the Palm Sunday parade is not a word that calls us to join him in celebration. Ultimately, the word of the "Palm Sunday God" goes something like this: "I have not come as a Mighty God to meet you in your strength. I have come as a Crucified God to meet you in your weakness. I have come to meet you at the depth of your human suffering. I have come to meet you when you walk in the valley of the shadow of death. I have come to meet you when you stand at the very gates of hell. I have come to walk with you in your darkness. I have come to walk with you in the night that you might one day walk with me in the light. Amen."

------

1. Mary Ann Tolbert, *Sowing The Gospel* (Minneapolis: Fortress Press, 1989), pp. 114-115.

2. *Ibid.*, p. 119.

Mark 12:28-34

The narrative told in Part Two of Mark's Gospel, chapters 11-16, slows down and broadens out.

> *The narrative creates the impression that events occur within six days (11:1, 11, 12, 19; 14:1, 12, 17; 15:42). The closer to the crucifixion, the more the detail about time and place ... A full one-third of the narrative is devoted to a few days in Jesus' ministry; one-sixth is devoted to his last 2 hours. What happens in Jerusalem clearly overshadows everything that has taken place thus far.* [1]

We come, that is, to the heart of the matter for Mark — and the heart of the matter is Jesus' death. Part Two of Mark begins with the story of the entry into Jerusalem. Some have suggested that it would be better to talk about Jesus' entry to the *temple*. Jesus sets up with his disciples on the Mount of Olives a kind of base camp for his trips to the temple. In Mark 11:11 we read that Jesus entered Jerusalem and went to the temple. He's back again in 11:15 after cursing a fig tree (11:12-14). During this trip to the temple Jesus cleans house! "My house shall be called a house of prayer ..." Jesus shouts as he overturns the tables of the money changers (11:17). Coming out of the temple Peter notes that the fig tree cursed by Jesus has withered (11:20-21). The curse and death of the fig tree surround the story of the cleansing of the temple as a kind of commentary. As it is with the fig tree, so shall it be with the temple. Its days are numbered.

In 11:27 Jesus comes again to the temple and engages in a series of dialogues with Jewish leaders. Jesus has brought an end to a certain way of thinking about the temple. Now he will bring an end to many of the teachings of the time. Jesus overturns both temple and teachings in his days in Jerusalem. Structurally speaking, Jesus first deals with three questions raised by various groups from Jerusalem (11:27-33; 12:13-17; 12:18-27). Jewish leaders have questions about Jesus' authority, about taxes to Caesar and about resurrection. In the midst of these teachings Jesus tells the story of the Parable of the Tenants in the Vineyard. Those who hear it understand it to be told against them (12:12).

Then come three short teaching episodes. This week's text comes in this section of Mark. The teachings are about the greatest commandment of the law (12:28-34), the relation of the Messiah and David (12:35-37), and two examples of religious practice: one bad, one good (12:38-44). The issues raised in all of these stories are issues of interest to Jewish readers. "The questions are precisely the sort that would be of interest to Pharisaic Jews who had witnessed the destruction of the temple and its aftermath—and who believed Jesus to be the promised Messiah."[2]

The centrality of the temple to the stories of the Passion is also a primarily Jewish interest. We have pointed out above that Jesus made three trips to the temple. The matter does not end there, however. In Mark 13:1-2 Jesus predicts that the temple will be destroyed. Not one *stone* will be left on another *stone*. Might this be a reference to the biblical quotation at the end of the plot synopsis in 12:1-11, which quotes Psalm 118 about the *stone* that the builders rejected becoming the head of the corner? Jesus Christ is to be the *cornerstone* of the Israel that will emerge on the other side of the temple and on the other side of the tomb.

At his trial one of the accusations brought against Jesus is that he claimed he would destroy the temple (14:57-58). We remember as well that at the moment of his death the *curtain of the temple was torn in two*! It is important to note this central role of the temple in Part Two of Mark's Gospel. The texts appointed for this year *do not include* these temple matters in any central way. It might be well for our preaching the few texts from Part Two of Mark's Gospel to put the stories in their narrative context. These chapters are clearly designed to demonstrate that the Heir of the Vineyard has come to overturn the practices of the temple and many of the teachings of the Jewish tradition.

174

Our text for today fits into this greater context and particularly into the context of Jesus' teachings. The question put to Jesus by one of the scribes is: "Which commandment is the first of all?" We know, of course, that this is a trap. The scribe is seeking to entangle Jesus in an age-old controversy among the rabbis. As usual, Jesus' answer avoids the trap. He answers by quoting from the Hebrew Bible, Deuteronomy 6:4-5:

> *Hear, O Israel: the Lord is our God, the Lord is one. You shall love the Lord your God with all your heart, and with all your soul, and with all your might.*

Jesus gives more than is asked of him in this context. He proceeds to give the second greatest commandment as well: "You shall love your neighbor as yourself." We have in this reply of Jesus a kind of summary of all that he stands for. Jesus is the Sower of the Word who sows the seed in many kinds of soil. The seed that falls on good soil gives fruit thirty, sixty and a hundredfold. Surely Jesus' description of the first and second commandments is a description of what happens to the seed that falls on the good soil!

In a shocking turn the *scribe commends Jesus* for his correct answer. "You are not far from the kingdom of God," Jesus replies to the scribe. This would appear to mean that this scribe is very close to seeing a vision of God's commandments that transcends matters of the temple. The scribe says to Jesus that loving God and neighbor "... is much more important than all whole burnt offerings and sacrifices" (12:33). The rites and rituals of the temple are not the most important thing! The scribe answers wisely. He has seen very close to the heart of the matter of God's reign. Love God. Love neighbor. That is far more important than temples and things! These verses, too, touch on the demise of the temple that characterizes Part Two of Mark's Gospel.

Homiletical Directions
We have spoken above about the organizing role the temple plays in Part Two of Mark's Gospel. Story One for our sermon

might well be a quick review of Part Two of Mark and the role that the temple plays in this structure. The point of the story, of course, is that Jesus has come to replace the temple and to replace many of Israel's teachings as well. What we observe is Jesus coming into Jerusalem and immediately paying a quick visit to the temple (11:11). He comes again to the temple to cleanse it (11:15-25) and to engage in dialogue with the Jewish leaders (11:27-33). In 13:1-2 Jesus prophesies the end of the temple. In the hour of his dying the temple curtain is torn in two (15:38).

Story Two would highlight this week's appointed text. Here is a story about that which takes precedence over the temple! The scribe recognizes that Jesus' call to love God and neighbor is "… more important than all whole burnt offerings and sacrifices." Jesus' call to love God and neighbor is the heart of the matter in the kingdom that he brings near. The scribe is "not far from the kingdom" when he recognizes that there is something greater than the religion of his ancestors which was centered in the temple.

Story Three could relate the heart of the kingdom, loving God and neighbor, to the Parable of the Sower. People who love God and neighbor are bearing the fruit of the seed which the Sower has come to sow.

Biblical reference could also be made to the story of creation and the story of Mount Sinai. In the creation story, told in Genesis 2, we see the foundation of human life as having a vertical (love God) and a horizontal (love neighbor) dimension. The vertical dimension is symbolized by the tree of the knowledge of good and evil. Adam is not to eat of this tree. He is called to obedience to God at the very center of the garden, the very center of his life. Humans are created in *dependence upon God*. They are to fear and love God above all things. The symbol of the horizontal dimension is the problem of Adam's loneliness. God saw that it was not good for the human to be alone. God created a companion for Adam. God created Eve. Humans are created to live in close relationships to others. These vertical and horizontal relationships stand at the heart of God's creation. Jesus did not come to replace these realities! Jesus came to call us to live in love to God and love to others.

The story of Mount Sinai can be read as making the same point. Israel there received from God a kind of minimal list of "ten words" to live by. The Ten Words or Commandments have two dimensions. The first table of the Law is a vertical table. God's people are asked to *not*: have any "other gods before me"; make graven images; take God's name in vain; and *to* remember the Sabbath to keep it holy. The second table of the Law is about human relationships. We are called upon to *not*: dishonor our parents; kill; commit adultery; steal; or bear false witness. This was God's will before the temple was built. This is God's will after the temple is destroyed.

The conclusion of our sermon needs to deal with the issue of living this kind of life. The worst thing we could do is to send people home with the words "love God and love neighbor" ringing in their ears in such a way that they think this is a task they can do out of their own power. We need only remember the countless stories told of the rocky-ground disciples. We have no right to assume that, left to our own willpower, we will do any better job than the disciples did! Loving God and neighbor is truly the fruit of a life where the seed of God's word has been sown upon the good soil of the human heart. It is only in the ongoing work of the Sower, only in the ongoing work of his casting his seed upon our soil, that we can expect results thirtyfold, sixtyfold and a hundredfold. The conclusion of this sermon, therefore, ought to be an invitation to people to stay in touch with the work of the Sower. The Sower sows the word whenever and wherever we hear the story of Jesus told. Through scripture, witness, sermon and sacraments the Sower sows his word!

"I am here today to sow the seed in your hearts," says Jesus. "I am here today to turn your hearts of stone into good soil. I am here to make your life sprout forth thirty, sixty and a hundredfold. I am here to cause new fruit to break forth from the encrusted soil of your heart. I am here to cause you to live a life of love of God. I am here to cause you to live a life of love for your neighbor. Amen."

---

1. Donald H. Juel, *Mark* (Minneapolis: Fortress Press, 1990), p. 150.

2. *Ibid.*, p. 172.

Mark 12:38-44

This week's Gospel text skips only Mark 12:35-37 from the ending of the assigned lesson for the Twenty-fifth Sunday after Pentecost. Chapter 30 sets the context for Mark 12:35-37, 38-44. Jesus is answering questions in this section which would appear to be the kinds of questions that Pharisaic Jews who had witnessed the destruction of the temple and who believed Jesus to be the promised Messiah might ask. The issue in Mark 12:35-37 is that of the relationship between David of old, to whom the promise of an everlasting Messiah was made, and the One who would come, who proclaimed himself to be the Messiah. In addressing this question Jesus gives a kind of riddle that must be given final answer by his listeners: "... so how can he be his son?"

The key to Jesus' complicated argument is his assertion, through the quote from Psalm 110:1, that the Messiah will sit at the right hand of God. In this coded message Jesus points to the importance of the final days for the determination of the true character of the Messiah. The Messiah must die and be raised again in order to fulfill the promises made to David. As in Jesus' other teachings throughout this Gospel, it is *through the death of the Promised One* that God fulfills the promises made of old. The death of the Anointed One plays a major role in Mark's Gospel. The story of Mark is the story of the Crucified Messiah.

This week's appointed verses, 38-44, contain teachings on two different kinds of piety. There is, first of all, a false kind of piety. The scribes exemplify such piety. They want the best seats in the house as a reward for their piety. They want the places of honor. They devour widows and pray long prayers. The Hebrew Bible is filled with all kinds of admonitions that people ought to care for widows, aliens and orphans (Deuteronomy 10:18; 14:28-29; 24:1-22, and so forth). Piety that devours widows, therefore, is no piety

178

at all. Neither is this the kind of piety that we have just heard spoken of in vv. 28-34. True piety, on the other hand, is like the piety of the poor widow who put everything she had into the treasury. Out of her poverty she gave her all. The clearest analogy to this story is the story of the rich man in Mark 10:17-31. He knew all the commandments. He had kept them from his youth. He was sure that his pious life would qualify him for eternal life. But he lacked one thing. He couldn't give all his possessions to God's service. So the rich man leaves Jesus in exceeding sorrow. He is a clear contrast to the widow, who lacked nothing in relation to the service of God. She gave all and was filled with exceeding joy!

We have discussed in an earlier chapter that the rich man sent away by Jesus is an example of *thorny ground*. "Thorny ground" people are those "... who hear the word, and the lure of wealth, and the desire for other things come in and choke the word, and it yields nothing" (Mark 4:18-19). The widow, on the other hand, is clearly *good soil*. The word has come to life in her bearing fruit, "... thirty and sixty and a hundredfold" (Mark 4:20).

The story of the sorrowful rich man in Mark 10:17-31 ends with the familiar gospel saying: "But many who are first will be last, and the last will be first." This saying surely fits our two stories for this week as well. The scribes in all of their public piety will be *last*. The widow who gave her penny will be *first*. In the reign of God such upside down logic is quite common!

Homiletical Directions

We stand here with another one of those texts from Scripture which is absolutely embarrassing for many Christian Americans. There are Christians in America who teach that wealth will be the reward for the true life of faith. They will have to skip over this story as quickly and as quietly as possible. There are many Americans in America who teach that wealth is the sure sign of success in our culture. Such is always the temptation in a capitalistic culture. Acquiring capital is the name of the game. Those who acquire are those we often admire. They have made it! It is their pictures we see on television and in countless magazines. We don't see many pictures of widows, or of anyone else for that matter, who give their last penny away. (Mother Teresa is an exception to this rule!)

So this simple text is a bombshell. Do any of us dare let it speak with its radically different vision of society? If we are not prepared to speak of this story in a way that grates on the American conscience perhaps we should not preach it at all. This text means what it says after all! That's the problem.

We have mentioned the story of the rich man in Mark 10:17-31 as a story in narrative analogy with this week's story. This is clearly one move we can make for preaching. We can put these stories side by side and basically let them speak for themselves. In the reign of God it is simply the case that by the world's standards the "first will be last and the last first." In the reign of God the rich man who has kept all the commandments is finally just so much *thorny ground,* while the widow with nothing is *good soil.* It may not be possible to explain this! Jesus doesn't explain it. He just tells the stories. We can do the same. Just tell the stories and let the Holy Spirit work through them in order to change the consciousness of those who hear. It may be that consciousness gets changed more through the simple juxtaposition of stories than it does through word upon word of didactic explanation.

The widow who gives her last penny is another of the "little people" in Mark who are the great heroes and heroines of the faith. This reality certainly suggests approaches to this text which are not based on telling Markan stories alone. As pastors we are well aware of the "little people" in our congregations who approach the widow's zeal in giving or in other areas of service of the gospel. Perhaps we should celebrate this Sunday as "little people" Sunday. Tell the story of the widow as the "matron saint of the 'little people.'" Then tell contemporary stories of "little people." "The first shall be last and the last first" can be the theme of such story telling if we desire to have a theme. A central theme may not be necessary in this case. Just let the stories speak for themselves.

Mark 13:1-8

In his work on Mark's Gospel, *A Master of Surprise,* Donald Juel joins an earlier argument made by R. H. Lightfoot on the context and nature of the material in Mark 13. Most biblical scholarship has labeled this chapter of Mark "Little Apocalypse." Lightfoot and Juel disagree with this label as they seek rather to discover the purpose of this material in Mark's greater narrative. Lightfoot argued that the material in Mark 13 served a function similar to the Parable of the Sower in Mark 4. The Parable of the Sower, according to Lightfoot, was to give assurance of the final, ultimate success of Christ's mission in spite of present obstacles. The Sower's seed will bear fruit! Juel quotes Lightfoot:

> *Probably the purpose of chapter 13 is largely similar, but now the horizon is far wider, and the surrounding darkness also very much greater. Chapter 13 is a great divine prophecy of the ultimate salvation of the elect after and indeed through unprecedented and unspeakable suffering, trouble, and disaster.[1]*

The Parable of the Sower promises that harvest and new birth will spring forth from the work of the Sower. This same kind of hope is present in the teachings of Jesus in chapter 13. There will be great trials and tribulation but in the end there will be harvest and new birth (Mark 13:24-27).

Juel continues to follow Lightfoot in his contention that the function of this narrative in Mark's Gospel is to serve as an introduction to the Passion Story. "He who is now reviled, rejected, and condemned is none the less the supernatural Son of man; and the terrible story of the last twenty-four hours has for its other side that eternal weight of glory which was reached and could only be reached, as the Church believed, through the Lord's death upon the cross, and through the sufferings of His disciples also."[2]

We spoke earlier of the organizing role that the temple plays in these first chapters of Part Two of Mark's Gospel (Mark 11-16). Jesus has made three journeys to the temple. He has debated with the temple's teachers over many issues. Through it all we sense the impending demise of the temple as the center of one's relationship to God. The scribe got it right when he responded to Jesus by saying that love of God and neighbor "... is more important than all whole burnt offerings and sacrifices" (Mark 12:28-34 [v. 33]). Temple practices are not as important as a life of dedication to God and neighbor. The widow with her penny is also a sign of the need for the temple's demise (Mark 12:38-44). The scribes, Jesus warns, devour widows! This poor widow put all that she had into the temple treasury. Such oppressive temple practices have to go.

These stories are the immediate introduction to Mark 13. In the first verses of Mark 13 we hear of the coming end of the temple. Jesus comes out of the temple *for the last time*. His disciples haven't figured out what these journeys of Jesus to the temple are all about. They still stand in awe of the place. "Look, Teacher," they say, "what large stones and what large buildings!" In response to their misplaced wonder Jesus speaks the final word about this religious institution: "Do you see these great buildings? Not one stone will be left here upon another; all will be thrown down" (Mark 13:1-2). And so it will be. In actuality the temple was destroyed by the Romans in 70 A.D. This fact was known, of course, by Mark's readers. The destruction of the temple *was a genuine religious crisis in Israel.* Chapter 13 may well be addressed primarily to this crisis! This chapter, that is, addresses an existential situation of the early church.

Mary Ann Tolbert hears in these opening words of Mark 13 strong echoes of the Parable of the Tenants in Mark 12:1-11. The owner of the vineyard will come finally and give the vineyard to others. In this way the stone that the builders rejected will become the head of the corner. The Beloved Son is killed by the wicked tenants. He is rejected. But his rejection by the wicked tenants prepares us for a new day when the rejected stone will be the true cornerstone. Temple stones will not be left standing. The cornerstone, however, will stand firm forever. In this almost coded language we are given to understand that Jesus has come to replace the temple as the focal point of the divine-human relationship. Relationship to God is founded in a rejected stone who becomes the head of the corner. This is the Lord's doing and it is marvelous in our eyes.

The inner core of the disciples (Peter, James, John and Andrew) inquires about the future. "Tell us, when will this be, and what will be the sign that all these things are about to be accomplished?" (Mark 13:4). Jesus gives answer to their question. Many of the signs of the end that he speaks of apply most directly to his own end. Again, this chapter serves as a kind of introduction to the Passion.

> *Jesus warns that they will "hand you over to councils" (13:9); he himself is handed over. He warns that his followers "will be beaten in synagogues"; Jesus must appear before Pilate where he is asked to testify on his own behalf. And "brother will betray brother to death," he tells them; one of his brothers, Judas, betrays him with a kiss (14:10, 43-46) ... While there is no one-to-one correspondence between Jesus' forecast and the ensuing narrative, there is enough to attract attention. The world for which he prepares his followers is precisely the world that has no room for him ... While the harvest lies ahead, what is of immediate concern are all the obstacles to growth.[3]*

All kinds of calamity will assault believers. Yet the metaphor is hopeful. "This is but the beginning of the *birth pangs*" (Mark 13:8). Birth pangs suggest that the new is on the horizon. There is a purpose in and through the trials of history. There is a purpose and there is a task we can busy ourselves with. "And the good news must first be proclaimed to all nations" (Mark 13:10). Sow the seed! That's what we do in the midst of the birth pangs. God will give the growth. The end of the matter is in the hand of the Lord of the Harvest!

Homiletical Directions

One way of setting today's story in narrative context is to tell the story of Mark 11 and 12 with a focus on the temple. (If you have already dealt with these temple passages in their overall context you will probably pass on this suggestion.) Tell the story of Jesus' journeys to the temple. Mark 11:1-11, the story of entry into Jerusalem, is really a story of entry into the temple (v. 11). On this trip Jesus just looks and leaves. His second journey to the temple is the time for cleansing (Mark 11:12-25). This trip to the temple is enfolded in the story of the cursing of the fig tree, which is a symbol of what must happen to the temple. The third journey to the temple is told beginning in 11:27. This journey is the occasion for many debates with the teachers of the temple. It is also the occasion for the second plot synopsis of Mark's Gospel — a parable which Jesus told and which the religious leaders took to be told against them! Both temple and teachers must fall. We indicated above how the verses in 12:28-34 and 12:38-44 prepare for the demise of the temple.

This week's Gospel text begins with Jesus leaving the temple for the last time. The disciples still stand in awe of this mighty building, but Jesus predicts that the day will come when not one stone of the temple will be left upon another. This is Jesus' climactic word against the temple.

We might next tell the plot synopsis story from Mark 12:1-11 if we haven't told it before. The focus in this telling is the climax of the story. The stone which the builders rejected has become the head of the corner! Jesus, not the temple, is the cornerstone, the very foundation of our faith.

We can allude next to the trials that will befall believers in the days that lie ahead. Mark 13 is full of such trials. As those whose lives are given alignment by the cornerstone, however, we can live in hope that the pains endured are really birth pangs of the reign of God. (See also Ephesians 2:17-22).

God's word to us through these stories is something like this: "I have sent my Beloved Son to earth but the wicked have killed him. Nevertheless, I tell you that my Son is the sure cornerstone of your life. Trials will come to you who build your life on the gift of my cornerstone. There will be wars and rumors of war. Kingdom will rise against kingdom. You will be persecuted in untold ways. Fear not. Stand firm on the stone which the builders have rejected. Stand firm in Jesus, my Son. I will bring you through the trials to new birth. I will bring you through the trials to eternal life in a kingdom which cannot be broken stone upon stone. I will bring you to a kingdom built on the eternal cornerstone: Jesus Christ. Amen."

Just a hint of another direction. Our first story would tell the text with a focus on the question of the disciples: "Tell us, when will this be, and what will be the sign that all these things are about to be accomplished?" This, after all, is a question that Christians ask in all ages. We want to know about the future. We want to know about the end-times. Many Christians are busy today telling all kinds of stories about the end-times that are wildly speculative. Jesus really puts an end to all such speculation when he says later in this chapter: "But about that day or hour no one knows, neither the angels in heaven, nor the Son, but only the Father" (Mark 13:32).

We don't know days and hours. We do know, however, what it is we are to be doing as we experience the birth pangs of the kingdom. We are to be Sowers of the Word! "... the good news must first be proclaimed to all nations" (Mark 13:10). From this reality in the story we can proceed to discuss ways in which we can be Sowers of the Word in our world today. Such a discussion will probably take more of a didactic form than a narrative form. This is so because the discussion is set up by the question of the disciples: "Tell us, when will this be, and what will be the sign that all these things are about to be accomplished?" Questions like that are still asked today. We can answer such questions in a teaching format.

---

1. Donald H. Juel, *A Master of Surprise: Mark Interpreted* (Minneapolis: Fortress Press, 1994), pp. 79-80.

2. *Ibid.*

3. *Ibid.*, pp. 84-85.

Mark 13:24-37

This week's Markan text comes near the end of Mark's Gospel, but it comes first in the Church Year. As such, this might well be the first chapter of this book that you read for sermon preparation. There are two Markan pericopes appointed from Mark 13. Mark 13:1-8 is discussed in the previous chapter, chapter 32. Please read this prior chapter before you work further on this week's Advent text assignment.

We pointed out in chapter 32 that Mark 13 might function in somewhat the same way that the Parable of the Sower functions in Mark's Gospel. The Parable of the Sower speaks to the issue of the failure of the kingdom-come-near-in-Jesus (Mark 1:15) to attract listeners. In chapters 2 and 3 of Mark we read of much controversey over Jesus' ministry and Jesus' rejection by the Pharisees and Herodians (Mark 3:1-6); by the scribes who had come down from Jerusalem (3:20-30); and by his own family (3:31-35). What is going on here? Will everyone reject the coming reign of God? The Parable of the Sower (Mark 4:1-34) says NO! There are a variety of kinds of hearers of the good news. There are "path" hearers and "rocky ground" hearers and "thorn" hearers, to be sure, but there are also those who will bear fruit thirty, sixty and a hundredfold. The kingdom of God, after all, is like a seed scattered on the ground that grows even if we don't know how it grows (4:26-29). The kingdom of God is like a grain of mustard seed that starts out very small but becomes the greatest of all shrubs (4:30-32). In other words, the kingdom of God will come but it will come through great rejection and trials.

Mark 13 sets the stage for the Passion story. The greatest tribulations are at hand! Here, as in Mark 4, the context is one of imminent failure. What will become of the One who promised to bring the kingdom near? The good news, of course, is that the kingdom will come! In the end, "... *they will see* 'the Son of Man coming in clouds' with great power and glory" (Mark 13:26). They will see! Seeing has been a problem for the followers of Jesus. (See Mark 4:12; 8:17-21.) The day is coming, however, when God will open blind eyes! Beyond the dark night of Jesus' passion and death will come a time when the light will burst forth from the darkness and the whole world will see! (See also Mark 14:61-62.)

The disciples had asked Jesus to tell them of the signs of the end (13:4). In 13:28-31 Jesus finally gets around to their question. The image he uses is that of a fig tree blooming in the summertime. Jesus' second trip to the temple is surrounded by a story about a fig tree which Jesus cursed (Mark 11:12-25). This fig tree is to die just as the religion of the temple had to die. The fig tree in Mark 13, however, is set to blossom forth into life. The image is a hopeful one.

There is hope also in the "words" of Jesus. "Heaven and earth will pass away, but my words will not pass away" (13:31). Jesus' *words* will not pass away. A dominant image for Jesus in the Gospel of Mark is that Jesus is the Sower of the Word. Throughout the chapters of this work we refer to Mary Ann Tolbert's suggestion that Mark 4:1-20 is the plot synopsis of chapters 1-10 of Mark's Gospel. The Sower sows the word (Mark 4:14). That's who Jesus is. We hear now that his sowing activity will never cease! It will overcome all obstacles. It will overcome even death and the grave. Everything else in heaven and earth might pass away. Jesus' words, the work of the Sower, will never pass away!

Mark 13:30 presents us with a difficulty. Jesus says that "... this generation will not pass away until all these things have taken place." Mark would appear to believe that these things would come quickly. Was he wrong? How are we to interpret such a passage? When we set this passage in its narrative context we see that many of "these things that would take place" actually happen to Jesus himself.

Jesus himself appears before the Sanhedrin and the governor. Judas, an insider and "brother," hands Jesus over to death. The sun is turned to darkness while Jesus hangs on the cross. These fulfillments do not mark the

end, but they demonstrate that Jesus' words are to be
*trusted. While **heaven and earth** will disintegrate, Jesus'*
promises will stand forever.[1]

The parable in this week's text (13:32-37) is a parable that calls upon the followers of Jesus to be faithful to their tasks in life and *keep awake* for the end! Juel argues that we get a glimpse here of the life of the early church. The early church was full of *sleepy believers*. Juel quotes his teacher, Nils Dahl, who argued that: "… the Gospel addresses a church that has tasted success and found it satisfying. It envisions believers who have taken the gospel for granted, who no longer see the world painted in dramatic colors. The story of Jesus is retold to shock them into awareness." [2] The risk of the early church was that they would just drift off. The upcoming episdode with Jesus and his disciples in Gethsemane (14:32-42) repeats much of the language of this parable. The disciples are to *keep awake*. But they fall *asleep*. They couldn't keep awake even *one hour*. The hour has *come* and Jesus is betrayed. Sleepy disciples portend a sleepy church!

Mark's Gospel is full of admonitions for our *eyes* and for our *ears*. When Jesus told the Parable of the Sower he began with an admonition: Listen! When he had finished the parable he said it again: Listen! (Mark 4:3, 9). But people do not listen. They do not understand. (We referred above to Mark 4:10-12; 8:17-21 which enunciates this theme.) "Listen," says Jesus. "Keep awake," says Jesus. Open your ears. Open your eyes. These are good Advent words!

Homiletical Directions

We might begin our story telling of this week's text by beginning at the end. Story One can be a retelling of the parable Jesus tells to close out this chapter of Mark. Tell it with elaboration to bring it into our contemporary world. The parable begins with the reality that no one knows the day or the hour of the end. Therefore we must keep alert. We might comment in passing that it is precisely the unknown hour of Jesus' coming that opens up the possibility of our salvation. If we knew the day and the hour we would all get ready! Jesus would come and ask us if we are ready and we would say: YES! And there is our downfall. We would find ourselves standing before Jesus Christ trusting in our own good works of preparation! But we don't know the day or the hour. We do know *who is coming*, however. We have met the future and his name is Jesus. We have met him in life as a gracious Savior. We shall meet him again on the last day and he will be for us there also, a gracious Savior.

It is interesting to note in this parable that the way people are to prepare for the coming is for "each with his work" to be faithful. One can almost see a doctrine of *vocation* here. In the light of the coming of the Son we are not supposed to do some kind of supraworldly religious things. We are to busy ourselves instead "each with his/her work." Life in the spirit of Jesus does not call upon us to leave this world but to love God and our neighbor "each with his/her work."

The telling of this story will end with a strong accent on the Son's call that we *keep awake*. We might note that this is an appropriate Advent theme!

Story Two would go to the tale of the disciples who *fall asleep* (Mark 14:32-42). Three times Jesus admonishes them to *keep awake*. Three times they fall asleep. You might want to make the point here that the *sleeping disciples* are a metaphor of the early Christian Church. People had grown contented. They had settled down comfortably in the faith. Jesus' strong call is to keep awake. It should not be difficult to let this story run quite naturally into the way things are among us today. Who among us ought not hear Jesus' word to keep awake? We are sleepers, and we live among people who are asleep as well to the energy of the reign of God. We are sinful people and we need to hear Jesus' stern word: Keep awake! This word is particularly fitting for the Advent season lest we sleep through it all overpowered, as it were, with its familiarity and spectacle. Keep awake!

The temptation is to end the sermon just here … just where Jesus ended. Keep awake! To end here, however, is to consign our hearers to life under the law. Do we have the power within us to keep awake? Our best models would surely be those closest to

Jesus. And what of those closest ones? They fell asleep. They could not see. They could not hear. They could not understand (Mark 8:17-21).

We need to end, rather, with a word of hope to sleeping believers. We can refer here to two parts of Mark 13. In 13:10 Jesus assures his disciples that the gospel will be preached to all nations. In 13:31 we hear that the words of Jesus will not pass away. You can tell here, as Story Three, the Parable of the Sower. Tell it with an emphasis on the fact that this parable is a metaphor for understanding Jesus as the One who Sows the Word. This sowing will never end. It will reach all nations (13:10). It will never pass away (13:31).

"I am the One who will Sow the Word forever," Jesus says to us through these stories. "I will sow the transforming power of the Word of God until every eye shall be open and until every ear shall hear. I will sow the word until your eyes are open and your hearts perceive. I will sow the word until your ears are open and your hearts understand. Listen! Watch! I am alive to wake you from your slumber and prepare you for eternal life. Amen."

---

1. Donald H. Juel, *Mark* (Minneapolis: Augsburg, 1990), p. 183.

2. Donald H. Juel, *A Master of Surprise* (Minneapolis: Fortress Press, 1994), p. 88.

Chapter 34
Passion Sunday

Mark 14:1—15:47

The Sunday of the Passion confronts us with a different kind of challenge. The appointed text is two chapters of Mark's Gospel. Mark's "passion narrative" is filled with narrative connections to the earlier chapters of his Gospel. Time after time throughout this work we have moved from Markan texts to sections of Mark 14 and 15 which stand in *narrative analogy* to them. The woman in Mark 14:3-9 who *breaks open an alabaster jar of ointment* is elsewhere in these chapters spoken of in analogy to the "tearing open of the heavens" (1:10) and the "tearing open" of the temple curtain (15:38). The fact that this woman understands that Jesus has come to die has been seen analogously to the disciples, who never did understand this reality. We might also note the narrative analogy between this story and the story of the resurrection. The story of Jesus' passion is surrounded (bookended) by stories of women anointing Jesus' body (Mark 14:8 and 16:1).

There is no way that we can begin to do justice to the narrative analogy that occurs in these chapters. Such a task might be useful if one were to preach on these chapters for a Lenten series. For a single Sunday, however, there is just too much going on here.

How shall we preach on such a lengthy and vital text? We cannot! Not in a single Sunday sermon. Our recommendation is that we find a variety of ways of telling this story to our people. Tell the story using a variety of art forms if possible. *Tell* it. Don't *explain* it! Let the story stand and work its own power. Let the Holy Spirit work with this powerful story, applying it to a variety of needs in the human hearts present for the telling.

Begin an annual tradition of telling this story on the Sunday of the Passion. Expand it each year until it fills the whole Sunday service. You will probably need to sit down with musicians, Sunday

191

School teachers, artists, dramatists and any other creative people in order to plan out a variety of ways of telling the heart of Mark's story.

There is a grand variety of ways in which this story can be told. It might begin with the "plot synopsis" of Part Two of Mark's Gospel (Mark 12:1-11) and proceed with Mark 14:1. Different storytelling approaches can be used for different parts of the story. One of the simplest ways of telling this story is to *memorize* parts of it for the telling. There is much power in biblical stories told in this way. What you should not do is *read* parts of the story. An exception here would be if you have a reader who can truly convey the drama of it all. That takes a person with some training in oral interpretation.

There are many ways of communicating these marvelous stories. Some of them have been set to music old and new. The masters have written wonderful Passion music that can be used in some places. There is good contemporary music as well. There are powerful pieces from *Jesus Christ Superstar,* for example. If you have a talented musician, some music could be written for the occasion. The hymnal has wonderful songs for some of the Passion events. In this way the congregation is a participant in the story telling.

You can use drama for some of the stories. Some would work well acted out by young people. Each Sunday School class could work on a portion of the whole. Children can also pantomime stories as they are told verbally. Adults, too, can take part in dramatic presentations. The trials of Peter and Jesus fit dramatic presentation very well (Mark 14:53-72). Use the Bible for your basic script. Both of these men are on trial. Jesus remains faithful when interrogated by a representative of the greatest power on earth. Peter is faithless when interrogated by a simple maid. These stories feed powerfully off each other.

These stories can also be put to choral readings. They can be rewritten in rap form. There are great films available on the days of the Passion. Use one or two film clips as a way to tell some of these stories. Use slides as a backdrop to some of the storytelling. Have an artist sketch scenes on a large sheet of paper. Use instrumental music as background music for many of the scenes. Artwork can be shown. Liturgical dance can be very effective. What is important is *to appeal to as many of our five senses as possible.* From watching television, our members are experienced at seeing and hearing several things at one time! Multi-media telling of stories, therefore, is also possible and perhaps even demanded by contemporary post-literate people.

As a backdrop to the work of telling these stories we shall hear a word from Werner Kelber about the tone of that which lies before us:

> *Mark's passion narrative is shrouded in darkness, gloom, and tragedy. More than in Matthew, Luke, and John, his is the story of an execution, of the victim's God-forsakenness, and of the demise of the victim's closest followers. There is an oppressive air hovering over the final days, and almost no relief from the horror of death. Divine intervention is not forthcoming during Jesus' hours of suffering ... There is ... no resurrection appearance to lighten up and overcome the anguish.[1]*

Donald Juel sets the scene like this:

> *There will be no spectacle, no escape from death. With one final cry, Jesus breathes out his spirit. The would-be-King is dead, his movement in shambles. He committed his cause to God, and God abandoned him ... Mark chooses to stress the incongruity, the scandal ... The only means of providing insight into the "reality" of such a story is by means of irony. Mark constructs a world in which a chasm separates reality from appearance ... He attempts in narrative form a "theology of the cross" — a glimpse of realty that takes as its point of departure the execution of the King of the Jews. If Jesus is the promised Messiah, this is how the world must be — and this is the only way the story can be told![2]*

Kelber and Juel help us find our way into the mood of these stories. We need to be faithful to this mood in our story telling. May God bless you and all who work with you in recreating the heart of the "greatest story ever told."

---

1. Werner H. Kelber, *Mark's Story of Jesus* (Philadelphia: Fortress Press, 1979), p. 71.

2. Donald H. Juel, *Mark* (Minneapolis: Augsburg, 1990), pp. 224-225.

Mark 16:1-8

We stand here at the climactic passage in Mark's Gospel. We should not be surprised to find that many of the stories from the earlier parts of the Gospel talk to this story in significant ways. There is much of *narrative analogy* here! This Easter tale begins with the women. These women have *names!* Many women have appeared in Mark's Gospel. Each one of them appears as a model of faithfulness: the woman with the flow of blood (5:24b-34); the Syrophoenician woman (7:24-30); the widow with her penny (12:41-44); and the woman who *broke open* the jar of ointment in order to anoint Jesus for burial (14:3-9). Models of faith these women are, *but they have no names.* The women who come to the tomb on Easter morning, however, *do have names.*

Mary Ann Tolbert finds these women to be very significant. They are *good soil* for the gospel. The impression left by these women is that they are a group far superior to the disciples. They are there at the tomb on this Sunday morning after all! Where are the disciples? "… these women appear to represent the good earth, that fruitful minority of humanity whose faithfulness demonstrates affinity with the kingdom of God."[1] We have high hopes for these women! Finally someone gets it right. We've had enough of the disciples, for goodness sake. But it shall not be so. Our hopes for these women rise throughout the Gospel until our hopes are dashed in the very last verse. The women fled from the tomb in terror and amazement, after all. *They were afraid!* "The seed has fallen on rocky ground once again, as fear, not faith, motivates their actions. Like the Twelve before them, the women too flee in silence."[2] We'll have more to say about this strange ending of Mark in the material that follows. Or is there a "lost ending" of Mark somewhere that will rehabilitate these women and these men?

Mary Magdalene, and Mary the mother of James, and Salome had bought and brought spices to anoint Jesus' body. The passion story of Jesus is surrounded by stories of women who anoint Jesus. (See also 14:3-9.) These tender stories of anointing surround the absolute godforsakenness of the story of Jesus' death.

The stone has been mysteriously rolled away from the tomb so that the women have easy access to Jesus' final resting place. They encounter there a kind of heavenly messenger who proclaims the incredible good news of Easter.

> *Do not be alarmed; you are looking for Jesus of Nazareth, who was crucified. He has been raised; he is not here. Look, there is the place they laid him. But go, tell his disciples and Peter that he is going ahead of you to Galilee; there you will see him, just as he told you.*
>
> (Mark 16:6-7)

The secret is out at last! At the end of the Parable of the Sower Jesus said: "For there is nothing hidden, except to be disclosed; nor is anything secret, except to come to light" (Mark 4:22). That which has been veiled in secrecy now comes to light. There will be no more calls for people to keep quiet about Jesus the Risen One. Now they can sow this good seed for all to hear. Now they know who he is. He could only be known through his dying and rising. Jesus had told them this consistently (8:31; 9:30-31; 10:32-34). The disciples totally failed to grasp the message Jesus proclaimed to them. Jesus is only finally revealed to them in his death! The disciples had not yet experienced this dying. How could they, therefore, see and hear, perceive and understand?

Mark's story is powerful at this point. Jesus is only known in the dying and the rising. Jesus is a Crucified Messiah. God raises this Son to new life. Resurrection confirms the cross as God's way in the world. This is a God present to all human crosses. And crosses we bear and will bear continually. But we bear our cross in hope. God is a God of the cross. God is a God who walks with us in our cross-marked lives. God is a God who ultimately lifts us from our cross to join God in Easter's new life.

The disciples are to meet Jesus in Galilee, "… as he told you." Jesus told them this in Mark 14:28: "… after I am raised up, I will go before you to Galilee." Jesus' promises are true! You can trust this Crucified Messiah! And you can go to work with this Crucified One. Galilee was the setting of the first 10 chapters of Mark's Gospel. Galilee was the land and the time of the Sower. The sowing must go on! (See Mark 13:10, 31.) This is Mark's version of a *great commission.* As disciples of the Crucified we are called upon to take up our cross (Mark 8:34-38) and go to Galilee and sow the word of God on every kind of human soil. The God who can raise Jesus from the *rock*-hewn tomb can also raise fruit from the *rocky ground* of the lives of the disciples and from the *rocky ground* of our hearts as well (Mark 4:5-6, 16-17). The God who raises the dead can enable us and all who hear the good news to bear fruit thirty, sixty and a hundredfold!

The commission to the disciples "to go to Galilee" is itself good news. We have followed Tolbert's lead in identifying the disciples as *rocky ground* kind of people. Three times in the boat stories they fail to grasp who Jesus is. Three times Jesus reveals to them that he must go to Jerusalem and die and be raised. He spoke to them of his cross. They continued to ask to share in his glory. Three times they fell asleep in the Garden of Gethsemane. Three times Peter denied his Lord. And yet it is just these people who are to go to Galilee to meet Jesus and to be on with the business of sowing the seed of the gospel. Surely there is hope for us all in this story!

The women again. At the tomb. The final words of Mark's story are about the *fear* of these women. *And they were afraid!* Throughout this study we have contrasted two responses to Jesus. People either *fear* or *believe.* The first passage to raise the issue of faith or fear as a response to Jesus is Mark 4:35-41, v. 40. (See chapter 14.) This theme is raised repeatedly throughout this Gospel. (See, for example, Mark 5:15, 33-34, 36.) The women at the tomb present us with the real possibility of a group of disciples who have *faith.* To find out in the last verse of the story that they, too, were *afraid* is a serious jolt to the reader. We had hoped so much that they would be different from the others. We had so hoped that in light of an empty tomb *faith* would be inevitable.

197

And what about this ending? You will find much material on this matter in any good Markan commentary. The issue in a narrative reading of the Gospel is really a question of how this ending functions in the story as a whole.

> ... we need to ask, not what this ending **means**, but what it **does** ... It is intended to move its hearers to respond, to excite their emotions on behalf of Jesus and the gospel message ... If the women frustrate the hope of the authorial audience for individuals to prove faithful to the courageous example of Jesus and follow his way by going out and sowing the word abroad, is there anyone else available to fulfill that task? ... Of course there is: the audience itself ... Each individual who hears the word sown by the Gospel of Mark ... is given the opportunity — as have all the characters in the story — to respond in faith or fear ... In the end, Mark's Gospel purposely leaves each reader or hearer with the urgent and disturbing question: What type of earth am I? Will I go and tell? [3]

Donald Juel puts the matter just a bit differently:

> Mark's Gospel forbids precisely that closure. There is no stone at the mouth of the tomb. Jesus is out, on the loose, on the same side of the door as the women and the readers. The story cannot contain the promises ... The doors in Mark's Gospel are emphatically open. The curtain of the Temple is rent asunder ... and the stone is rolled back from the tomb ... Jesus is out of the tomb; God is no longer safely behind the curtain. [4]

The first time I ever experienced the book of Mark as a complete narrated event was when I heard it told by David Rhoads. That was when I received insight into the so-called "lost ending" of Mark. It was absolutely clear to me that this Gospel story did not end in Mark 16:8, "and they were afraid." This Gospel story would only end in my heart! This Gospel story will only end in your heart as well. Herein lies a fundamental key for preaching this Easter story in Mark's key. The story should end in the hearts of all who hear us preach. Fear or faith? How shall it be with us?

Homiletical Directions

There are many directions possible for preaching on this climactic word from Mark. You are invited to follow any of the leads given above. The single possibility we shall suggest is that we follow these women! Story One might be the story of the failure of the disciples. This story begins in Mark 4:35-41. The disciples are in the boat with Jesus and a great storm arises. They cry out to Jesus to help them. Jesus helps! And he wonders why they were *afraid.* They do not believe. The next time they are in the boat with Jesus they again demonstrate their *fear* (Mark 6:45-52). Fear is not mentioned in the third boat scene, but again we see the disciples' total lack of understanding (Mark 8:13-21). We have just come through Holy Week and we have been reminded again, in a threefold way, of the lack of faith of the disciples. Jesus tells them to stay awake and they fall asleep (Mark 14:32-42). The important thing in telling stories of the disciples is to establish *fear* as their fundamental response to Jesus.

Story Two might walk back through the stories of some wonderful women in Mark's Gospel. We behold the *faith* of the woman with a flow of blood (Mark 5:33-34). Though the word "faith" is not used it is certainly implied in the story of the Syrophoenician woman (Mark 7:24-30). *Faith* would appear to be the hallmark as well of the woman at Bethany who anointed Jesus beforehand for his burial (Mark 14:3-9). Disciples fear. Unnamed women believe! That's the flow of the story.

The *faith* of these *unnamed* women is remarkable. We are prepared for the best, therefore, when we meet the *named women* in the Easter story. This is Story Three. We anticipate the best from these women. Tell Mark 16 with emphasis on our hopes for these women. They are there. The disciples are not. Surely they will believe. But no. The story ends on a most unsettling note. *They were afraid.*

In conclusion to this sermon we should lift up again these possible responses to Jesus: fear or faith. We should point out that this ending of Mark's Gospel *does* something very interesting. If the disciples fear and the women fear, who is left to *have faith*? The answer, of course, is that *we are!* The Gospel of Mark ends in our hearts as we respond to the words of the heavenly messenger. The final words of this sermon could well be the words of the heavenly messenger now addressed to us. In the story they were addressed to the women and they responded in *fear.*

"Now, therefore, hear these words as words addressed to you today. Let them echo in your heart. How shall you respond to them? 'Do not be alarmed; you are looking for Jesus of Nazareth, who was crucified. He has been raised; he is not here. Look, there is the place they laid him. But go, tell his disciples and Peter that he is going ahead of you to Galilee; there you will see him, just as he told you.' "

The sermon should end just there with its challenge to the human heart. It might be wise to repeat these exact words a second time. Now you have sown the word. Let there be a moment or two of silence for the words to sink in. Then lead your people in prayer that the Risen Christ might arise in our hearts empowering us to *faith.*

---

1. Mary Ann Tolbert, *Sowing the Gospel* (Minneapolis: Fortress Press, 1989), p. 292.

2. *Ibid.*, p. 295.

3. *Ibid.*, pp. 295-299.

4. Donald H. Juel, *A Master of Surprise* (Minneapolis: Fortress Press, 1994), p. 120.